Welcome

Stuart Andrews is a technology journalist specialising in PCs, games and business and educational IT. He writes for a range of computing and technology magazines and websites, including *ICT Reviews*, *PC Pro*, *Cloud Pro*, *ComputerActive*, *TrustedReviews* and *The Sunday Times*. His first computer was a Sinclair ZX Spectrum, but he now uses a range of tablets, Chromebooks and Windows 8 PCs, none of which have rubber keys. You can follow him on Twitter at @SATAndrews.

Andrew Dixon has been teaching ICT for eight years. A Computer Science graduate, he's always had a passion for the unlikely combination of programming and playing rock guitar. He is currently Head of ICT and Computing at Summerhill School in the West Midlands and was nominated for Teacher of the Year in 2009. A self-confessed coding geek and gadget junkie, Andrew is always pursuing new and emerging technologies in education and writes regularly for *ICT Reviews* and *PC Pro*. You can follow him on Twitter at @ADXeventide.

Many of the projects in this book use Scratch. Scratch is developed by the Lifelong Kindergarten Group at the MIT Media Lab. See scratch.mit.edu

Anyone can code. Certainly, writing the next Minecraft or programming complex simulations from scratch will require a deeper knowledge, but anyone and everyone has the potential to learn some basic coding skills, then take those skills and write a simple program. This book can help you and your kids take that potential further. Read it, follow the projects and get to grips with the fundamentals of programming, and you and they can learn to code.

We live in a world where technology and everyday life have never been more tightly interwoven, and that technology – the hardware, websites and services we use all the time – is dependent on software. An understanding of how that software is made is as valuable in the 21st century as an understanding of engineering was in the 19th and 20th, and it's only going to grow more important.

Forget all that stuff of grave importance, though, or you may miss the fact that coding can be fun. You can make something in less than an hour, watch it work, then go back and make it better. As long as you have a computer – and almost any laptop or PC will do – you can build something brilliant, bizarre or even useful, and the tools won't cost you a penny. Coding is creative. It pushes your imagination, your ability to improvise and your ability to plan.

Most of all, it doesn't have to be difficult. In this book, we'll show you how you can use visual tools such as Scratch to build programs object by object or block by block, so that kids as young as seven or eight can make their own funny animations or playable arcade games. While they're doing it, they'll absorb fundamental concepts that will help them develop their skills later on. We also introduce SmallBASIC – a simplified version of the classic coding language, which is free to use and surprisingly easy to learn. By the time this book is over, we'll have started using Visual Basic, a tool that many professional programmers use every day.

The projects in this book are fun, so that kids and adults will enjoy making them, and playing them once they're done. They're also easy to customise, so that novice programmers can take what we've put together, change it and make their own mark. That's important, because programming isn't about using technology, but about taking it apart, seeing how it works and making it better. We hope that you and your kids will take these projects, improve them and make them your own. There's no better start on a programmer's journey.

Stuart Andrews
Editor

Contents

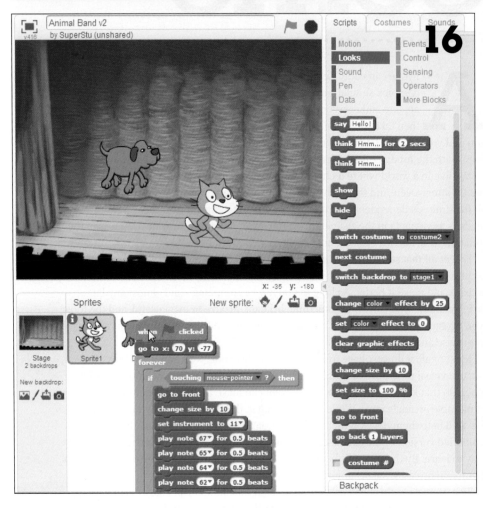

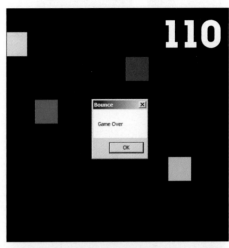

Chapter

1

Section 1
Start coding

The ability to program has never been as important as it is right now. In a digital age, an understanding of code and how it works is an incredibly useful skill. It can transform you from someone who uses other people's software into someone who can make it. It can help you get to grips with real computing, and it can be a fun and interesting pastime. It might even one day help you get a job. Right now, this knowledge might seem out of reach, but with the aid of the projects on the next few pages and an easy, graphical programming tool called Scratch, we're going to help you through the fundamental concepts, and steadily teach you how to code. Before you even know it, you'll have taken your first steps into a world of programming and be hungry for more.

IN THIS SECTION

Why learn to code?

In a digital age, being able to code has become a vital skill. Discover how to create something brilliant using just a PC, a screen and free software

Code is everywhere, and not just where you might think. When you're running apps on a smartphone or playing games on a console, it seems obvious that the app you're using or the game you're playing has been put together by programmers, using lines of code to stitch together every last feature, every button you tap and everything you see on the screen, so that it all does the job it's meant to do.

This is why learning to code is important. It can take you from someone who can use technology to someone who can create technology or make amazing things with it. It could also be the passport to an incredible future. You could one day be helping to build the next iPhone, create a blockbuster film or help a Formula One racing team make faster cars, all by using your coding skills.

Most importantly, coding can be fun. Often, you're creating something brilliant from nothing, using just a computer, a screen and some free software. Change something in your program and you can see

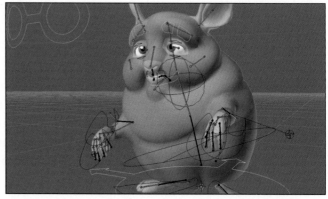

▲ Computer-generated movies exist because programmers developed the software to produce them, and work with artists to code more lifelike or advanced effects. Blender is a free 3D graphics package, developed by hundreds of programmers working together.

the result on the screen, and it's pretty hard to make any mistakes that you won't be able to fix. Coding can be like solving a puzzle. You know what you want to do, or that something isn't working properly, and it's exciting to find a way to make it better. Whatever you're doing, you can do something brilliant, and make it your own.

What can this book do to help?

This isn't one of those books that tells you all about programming but not how to do it. Nor is it one of those books that gives you lots of code to type in, but doesn't tell you how it works or what it's doing. Instead, we're going to take you through a series of projects that will introduce the most important concepts, help you use the key building blocks of code, and enable you to create fun programs that you can then go back and change. We're going to start off easy and slowly add the more complex

WHAT IS CODING?

When it comes to computing, code means a set of written instructions for a computer, usually arranged in a structure called a program. When a user runs the program, the code tells the computer what to show on the screen, how to process any data that the program uses, and what to do if certain things happen; for example, if a button is pressed. Programming – or coding

– is the art of writing those instructions so that the computer can understand them, and the program functions as it should. It's also the art of arranging those instructions so that the program works as smoothly and as quickly as it can, and doing all this in a way that other programmers can follow if they need to look at or change your code.

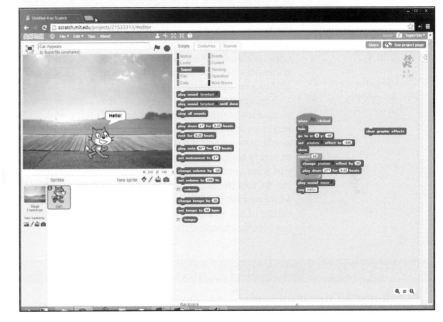

◄ Without programmers, we wouldn't have amazing games like Minecraft. Learn to code, and you might help create the next big gaming hit.

66 You might start as the young apprentice, but you'll finish feeling like a coding Jedi Master 99

stuff, so that you're never left drowning in a sea of jargon, or having your mind boggled by big chunks of code that make your eyes and brain hurt. You can start the book knowing almost nothing, but by the end you'll feel confident enough to explore the world of coding further. You might start as the young apprentice, but you'll finish feeling like a coding Jedi Master.

The projects are designed so that they can be completed by younger children with a little parental help, or by older children working on their own.

How does it work?

Our projects kick off with Scratch – a highly visual, easy-to-use programming tool that was designed to introduce the main concepts of programming, and help young novice coders build something good with minimum fuss. We'll then move onto SmallBASIC, a refined version of the classic coding language, designed to get young programmers used to working

▲ Coding doesn't have to be difficult. Use easy tools like MIT's Scratch, and almost anyone can do it.

with a proper text-based programming environment. Finally, we'll look at projects that use Visual Basic Express – a free version of the same tool being used by millions of professional programmers around the world.

Along the way, we'll tell you what you're going to learn, take each project apart, and pick out all the vital bits of code that make the program work as it should, or that you might want to come back to and change later on. After all, these aren't our fully finished projects – they're starting points for your own. ●

Introducing Scratch

With a drag-and-drop approach, Scratch is the perfect way to start coding

Originally developed by computer scientists at America's Massachusetts Institute of Technology (MIT), Scratch is a simple, visual programming language that you can use to create cartoon animations, interactive stories and simple games. It's designed for kids aged eight to 16, but it's a good way for someone of any age to learn the basics of programming. While a Scratch program might not look like what you'd think of as a program, with its chunky blocks you drag and click together, it still works like one and uses the basic parts that you'd find in a real program.

The great thing about Scratch is that it takes away a lot of the complexity of programming and leaves you free to think about how the program needs to work and what it needs to do. You don't need to worry about writing your code in the right way so that your computer can understand it. You just drag blocks into the Scripts space and click them together, a bit like blocks of Lego. Make a mistake and put things in the wrong order, and you can easily separate the blocks, change, delete or move them around.

▲ Scratch projects are designed for sharing. You can try other people's, and transform them with your own 'remix' projects.

It's hard to imagine a more intuitive way to code.

Scratch doesn't just give you all the building blocks for a program, but also a whole grab-bag of great stuff that you can use in them. You'll find a wide range of cartoon characters to star in your program – everything from dogs and dinosaurs to ghosts, aliens and penguins. You'll find a selection of background scenery, and a library of musical instruments, drums and sound effects. And if Scratch doesn't have what you're looking for, it's easy to import your own stuff from your computer or use the simple, built-in tools to make new characters, scenes and sounds.

The other great thing about Scratch is that you don't have to learn on your own. The Scratch website (scratch.mit.edu/) is the centre of a huge community, where you can try other users' programs or get help, hints and tips on making your own. It's also where you can eventually share your own programs, so that when you've made something that you're proud of you can let your friends and family try it out. Plus, with millions of Scratch users out there, you could make a name for yourself as a Scratch coding superstar! ●

ABOUT SPRITES

The most important things in any Scratch project are the sprites. Sprites are the characters or objects that move around or do things in your program. They're the heroes and the villains, the actors in your cartoons, the cars and spaceships that you might set racing around. You program what the sprites do and when they do it by giving them instructions in scripts. These tell your sprites what to do and where to go, what to say or what noise to make. They also tell your sprite what to do when something happens – for instance, when it hits another sprite.

The default sprite – the one that automatically appears in any new project – is the Scratch cat, but he doesn't have to be the star of your program. You can use any sprite from the large library, or make your own. The great thing about sprites is that, once you've added one and built a script, you can duplicate it, change it and use it again in the same project, or even export it – make a copy and send it out of your project – so that you can use it in a completely different project.

Signing up for Scratch

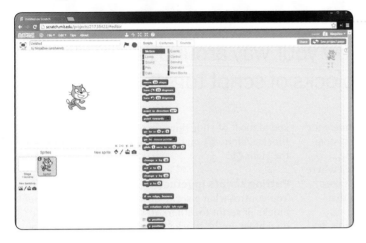

You don't need to install anything to start coding with Scratch. Switch on your computer, fire up your browser, and type scratch.mit.edu into the browser and the page loads. Click on the Create button or on the Try it Out button below, and the Scratch editor loads, complete with step-by-step instructions to try your first sample program.

STEP 2 To really get to grips with Scratch, though, you need to sign up. Click on the Join Scratch button in the bar at the top. Now, go to the window that pops up and choose a Scratch Username, then enter a password. You'll need to enter the same password in each of the two boxes to confirm it. Press Next.

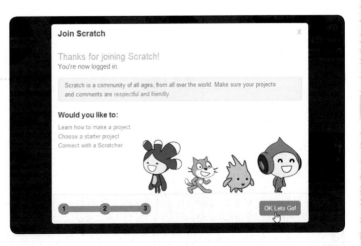

STEP 3 Now you need to enter the month when you were born and the year, your gender, the country where you live and an email address. This can be a parent's email address if you don't have one of your own. When you've entered all these things, click Next.

STEP 4 You're all signed up! Now it's time to get started. Under 'Would you like to:' on the left-hand side, you'll find links to take you to the sample program we mentioned earlier, choose a basic starter project to be getting on with, or get help and advice from the Scratch community's friendly Welcome Committee. The projects here do a nice job of explaining how to use Scratch, and how to behave while you're using it. Click the OK, Let's Go button to go back to the Scratch homepage, and start working on your first Scratch project.

Scratch basics

Scratch is very easy to use once you know your way around its simple interface and discover how to connect blocks of script together

WHAT YOU'LL LEARN

>> What the different parts of the Scratch inferface do

>> How to select instruction blocks and connect them in a stack

>> All about the Toolbar and the Costumes window

Two things make Scratch the perfect choice for novice programmers: its block-based system for building scripts, and its very simple, logical interface. The Stage ❶, the area where your project plays while you're working on it, takes up the top-left corner of the window. Beneath that sits the Backdrops area ❷, where you can add background scenery for the Stage, and the Sprites area ❸, where you add and delete your sprites, and select them for editing.

The right-hand side of the screen is where all the work really happens. It switches between three windows, covering Scripts, Costumes and Sounds, and you can flip between the three by clicking the tabs ❹ at the top of the area. Scripts is where you'll spend most of your time, dragging blocks from the Blocks Palette ❺ on the left into the Scripts area on the right ❻.

Putting scripts together

You control what a sprite does by connecting different blocks of script together. All you need to do is click on a block in the Blocks Palette, hold the left mouse button down, then drag it into the Scripts area and release the mouse button. Drag another block and release it just above or below the last one, and the two will join together in a stack. A white highlight above or below the block to which you're joining will tell you where the new block will go.

Stacks of script run from top to bottom, and once

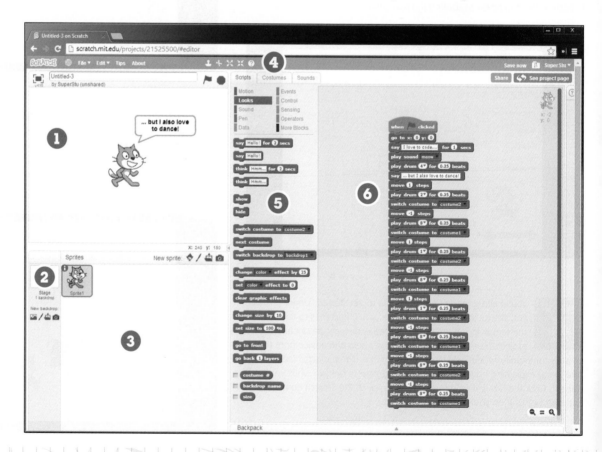

THE TOOLBAR

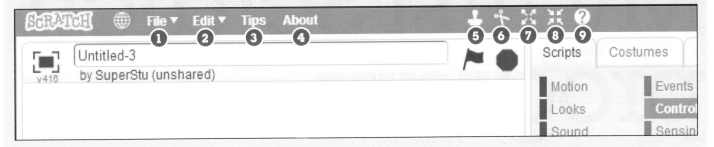

The Toolbar at the top of the screen has all the most important Scratch menus, plus some buttons you'll need to use while working on a project.

1 File: Clicking on File opens up a dropdown menu, with options to start a new Scratch project, save your current project, save your current project as a copy, go to the My Stuff page to look at other projects, upload a project you've saved on your computer, or download a project so that it's saved on your computer. The Revert option resets the whole project to the state it was in when you launched Scratch and opened it. It's a useful option if you've made a total mess of things, but use it carefully as you could lose hours of work!

2 Edit: The Undelete option is the biggie here. Scratch makes it a bit too easy to delete a huge block of instructions in one go. If you do it accidentally, you'll need to click Edit then Undelete to bring it back. The Small Stage Layout

option offers you a different interface that gives you more space for the Scripts area. This can be useful when you're working on a complex project, and you can always click it again to go back to the normal layout. The Turbo mode option runs your project at a faster speed. You can switch it on and off by clicking it again.

3 Tips: Opens up a Tips window, with a couple of built-in step-by-step project walkthroughs, and advice on the different types of block and what they all do.

4 About: Takes you to the About Scratch webpage, which tells you more about Scratch and how to use it.

5 Duplicate: Click on this and your mouse pointer becomes a rubber stamp. Clicking on a Sprite on the Stage will create an exact duplicate, complete with costumes and scripts. Clicking on a block of script in the Script area will make another copy of the block. You can

also duplicate sprites and blocks by right-clicking on them and then left-clicking Duplicate in the menu.

6 Delete: Click on this and your pointer becomes a pair of scissors. Clicking on a Sprite will now delete it, and the same goes for a block of script in the Script area. You can also delete sprites and blocks by right-clicking on them, then left-clicking Delete in the menu.

7 Grow: Click on this button, then click on a sprite in the Stage window, and it will grow bigger.

8 Shrink: Click on this button, then click on a sprite in the Stage window, and it will get smaller.

9 Block Help: Click here, then click on a block in the Blocks Palette or Script area. A tips window will appear, telling you what it is and how it works – a helpful reminder.

they're joined they stay joined unless you click and drag a block down away from the block above. When you do that, any blocks joined to it at the bottom will move away at the same time. This is important when it comes to deleting or replacing an individual block. If you don't drag it away from the blocks above, then drag away the blocks below, you'll delete every block in the script.

You can switch between the different types of block by clicking on the categories – Motion, Looks, Sound and the rest – at the top of the Blocks Palette. Click on Control and you'll notice that some blocks have a kind of C or E shape. These blocks are designed to work closely with other blocks and change what they do, and will fit in above and below existing blocks. Just drag them into the Scripts area, but watch the white highlights to see where they'll slot in. And when you add blocks to a C- or E-shaped control block, watch the highlights to check that they're going to fit in the right place. ●

THE COSTUMES WINDOW

Clicking on the Costumes tab opens the Costumes window. Costumes allow you to clothe your sprites with different graphics, so that you can have different frames, to make your sprite look like its walking or running, or different expressions, to make it look happy, sad, angry or frightened. Existing Costumes for the current sprite are listed on the left **1**, or you can add your own Costumes from the library

2, from a camera **3**, or by painting your own in the Costume editor **4**. You can also use the Costume editor to change the existing Costumes (we'll talk about this in more detail later on).

My first Scratch program

It's time to write your very first Scratch program, and make the Scratch cat magically appear using some simple but fun effects

WHAT YOU'LL LEARN

- How to build a simple Scratch script
- How to bring in backdrops
- About simple visual effects
- How to use loops in a Scratch program

TOP TIP
To save a Scratch project, type a name into the textbox above the Stage area, then click on File to open the File menu and click Save Now.

For our first program, we're going to keep things simple. We'll use the Cat1 sprite that appears with every new Scratch project, and we'll do nothing more complex than add a background and drag a few blocks into place.

STEP 1 Our leading actor today is the ever-friendly Scratch cat. He wants to say 'Hello!' Click on the Looks category in the Blocks Palette, then drag and drop the Say Hello! Block into the Scripts area. Click on the block, and the cat will say 'Hello' from the Stage.

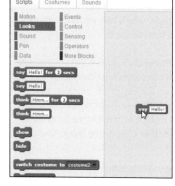

STEP 2 Now go to the Events block and drag the When Clicked block with the picture of the green flag so that it sits on top of the 'say Hello' block. Press the red Stop button above

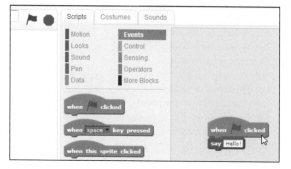

the Stage, then the green Go flag. You've just written your first program, and clicking the green flag starts it running.

STEP 3 You've got a friendly cat, but not the most interesting program. Let's add a backdrop to give our feline friend some scenery. Go the Backdrop area to the left of the Sprites area, and click on the 'Choose new backdrop from library' option. Click on the beach Malibu picture, and click OK. The new background is a start, but let's make things a bit more exciting.

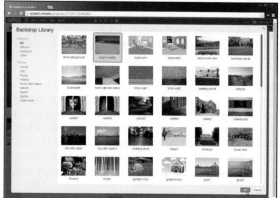

STEP 4 How about a cat that magically appears on the beach? Click on the Scripts tab, then drag the 'say Hello!' block away from the green flag block, and leave it somewhere at the

bottom of the area. Now click on the Looks category in the Blocks Palette, and drag the block that says 'set color effect to 0' into place beneath the green flag block.

STEP 5
Where a block has an arrow on it, it means there's more than one option. Click on the arrow, and select Pixelate from the list of effects. Now we need to change the strength of the effect. Click on the white area with the number in it, and type in -250.

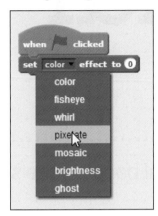

STEP 6
Now for the clever bit. Drag the 'change color effect by 25' block from the Blocks Palette and place it underneath your existing blocks. Change the effect from 'color' to 'pixelate'. This will start transforming your cat from a blocky mess into his old feline form. A sound effect adds to the fun, and makes the change take a little longer. Click on the Sound category and drag the 'play drum 1 for 0.25 beats' block into place.

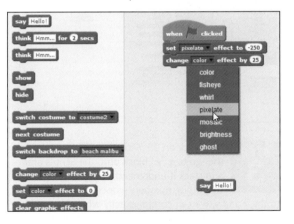

MESS AROUND

Your cat doesn't have to say 'Hello'. Click on the white box next to 'say' on the purple block and you can type in anything you like. Try changing the drum noise in step 7 to different sounds, and try changing the duration (the number before the beats) to different values, like 0.1 or 0.5. See how the project works with different effects, like whirl or ghost. Just remember to alter the setting in both the Set and Change purple blocks, and change the strength of the effect to see what that does. Make the cat appear your way!

LOOPS

When you use the Repeat block, you're creating a loop. Loops are one of the most common structures you'll find in a program. They tell the computer to keep on doing something until a certain condition is reached – in this case, until the loop has run ten times.

Using loops is a good way to keep your program working at a repetitive task without having to keep adding the same instructions yourself. In more complex programs, they play a large part in controlling how the program and the different parts of it behave.

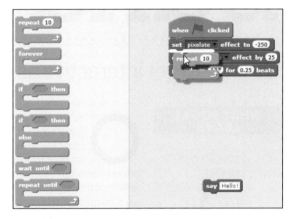

STEP 7
Click the arrow next to drum 1 and select drum 17, the Vibraslap. Now, we could just keep adding the last two blocks, doing so ten times over to bring the cat back to normal (as that's how many steps it would take to turn the Pixelate effect from -250 to 0). Luckily, there's a quicker way. Click on the Control category in the Blocks Palette, then drag the 'repeat 10' block to the Scripts area and drop it in below the first 'set pixelate...' block.

STEP 8
Now grab the 'change Pixelate effect...' block and drop it inside the C of the 'repeat' block. See how the 'Play drum...' block comes with it? Drop it in place, then drag the 'say Hello!' block up again so that it connects to the rest of the program. You're program is done! Press the green flag above the Stage to see it in action. ●

The animal band

It's time to get interactive as you put an animal band on the stage

Our first Scratch program was fun, but it wasn't very clever or interactive. The most useful and interesting programs involve interaction – they respond to an action from the user, whether that's moving the mouse, tapping a key on the keyboard or clicking on a button on the screen. That's why our next project goes a little deeper, with a musical bunch of animals, all primed and ready to perform at the first touch of the pointer.

STEP 1
This time we'll start with a backdrop. Go to the Backdrop area next to the Sprites area, and click on the 'Choose backdrop from library' button. Scroll down until you can see the Stage backdrop with the red curtain, then click to select it and press OK. The stage is here, and with Scratch cat on the boards it already has our first performer.

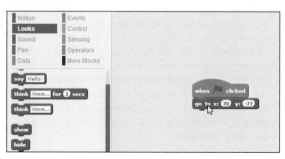

STEP 2
Let's make sure our first musician hits the right spot every time. Click on the Scratch cat sprite in the Sprites area to select it. Now click on the Scripts tab, then the Events category. Drag the 'when green flag clicked' block from the Blocks Palette and drop it onto the Scripts area.

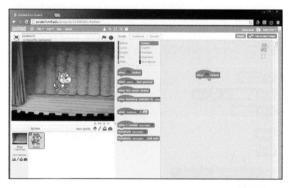

STEP 3
Now click on the Motion category and drag the 'go to x: y:' block onto the Scripts area and stack it underneath the green flag block. By putting numbers – or coordinates – next to the x and y, we can control exactly where the cat appears on stage. Here, click on the number next to x and type 70, then click on the number next to the y and type -77. Click on the block, and our cat moves into the right position.

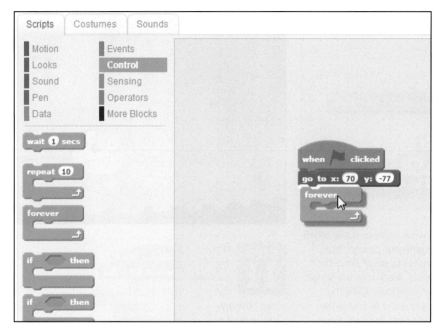

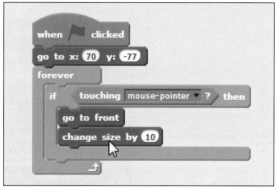

STEP 4

Now for the interactive bit. Click on the Control category, then drag the 'forever' block onto the Scripts area and connect it at the bottom. The 'forever' block keeps running the blocks inside it over and over, no matter what else is happening in the script. We're going to use it to make sure this script keeps looking for our user to interact with the program.

STEP 7

Our script is now looking to see whether the mouse pointer touches the sprite, so we need to tell it what to do when that happens. First, a simple visual effect. Click on the Looks category, and drag the 'go to front' block, then the 'change size by 10' block into the C shape of the 'if then' block.

STEP 5

Grab the 'if x then x' block from the Blocks Palette and drop it inside the C of the 'forever' block. The 'if x then x' block tells the script that if a certain 'thing' happens, it's to do whatever instructions we give it inside the C of the block. We'll define what that 'thing' is in the next step.

STEP 8

It's time to get our star making music. Click on the Sound category, drag the 'set instrument to x' to block onto the Scripts area, and drop it right beneath the 'change size by x' block. Again, watch the highlight to make sure it's going in the right place. Click on the arrow next to the 1 and set the instrument to 11, the Saxophone.

STEP 6

Click the Sensing category, then drag the 'touching' block and drop it onto the little slot between the 'if' and 'then' of the 'if then' block. You have to be careful here, so watch for the highlight to make sure it's going in the right place. Click the arrow next to the question mark, and select 'mouse-pointer' from the dropdown menu.

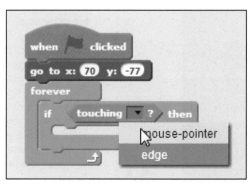

17

STEP 9

That tells the script what noise to make when we touch the sprite with our pointer, but what about which notes to play? Drag the 'play note x for x beats' block into the Scripts area and stack it underneath the last block. Click the arrow next to the first number, and set it to 67, or the musical note G. Leave the number next to beats alone for now.

STEP 10

Repeat that last step three more times, stacking each 'play note x for x beats' block below the last. Now go through and change the values for each note to 65, 64 and 62. This sets our cat saxophonist to play four notes of a simple downward scale.

STEP 11

If you try running the script now, by clicking on it or clicking the green flag, you'll notice that our cat keeps getting bigger. Let's stop that once he's played his piece. Click on the Looks category, then drag the 'set size to x%' block and the 'go back x layers' block in beneath the 'notes' blocks, but still within the C shape of the 'if then' block. Set the number in the first block to 100 and keep the number in the second to 1.

STEP 12

That's one band member sorted, but we need to add some others. Go to the Sprites area and click the 'Choose sprite from library' button next to New Sprite. Select the Dog2

TOP TIP
ASSIGNING VALUES
In Scratch, many blocks work with values – a number you type in or select from a menu that controls how the block behaves. Many will have a ready-set value, like 10 or 50, but for the purposes of the book we'll refer to these values as x or y. Altering the values can be a good way to experiment with a Scratch project. If you don't like what happens, just put the value back to what it was before.

COORDINATES

When Sprites need to go to a certain place or move around the Stage, we control where they go and what they do using coordinates. There are two coordinates for each position. The first, the x coordinate, tells the sprite where to go horizontally, or left and right along the Stage. The second, the y coordinate, tells the sprite where to go vertically, or up and down inside the Stage. x: 0, y: 0 is the centre of the Stage, so you use minus numbers when you want a Sprite to go left or down of centre, and positive numbers to place them up or right of centre. The same goes when you want them to move, which we'll look at later on.

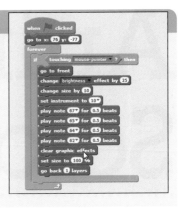

MESS AROUND

You can add any sprite you want to your band, and alter the instrument they play and the notes they play on it just by altering the values – the numbers – in the 'set instrument' block and 'play note' blocks. If you want, you can also add visual effects to your sprites so that they change colour or brightness when you touch them with the pointer. Just drag a 'change x effect by x' block into the stack beneath the 'go to front' block, then drag a 'clear graphic effects' block underneath the 'play note x for x beats' blocks.

sprite, then click OK. Hey presto, a dog appears on the stage.

STEP 13 At this point, you're probably thinking "Oh no, I've got to make a whole new script for the dog!" Actually, you don't. Click on the Cat sprite, then right-click on the block of script and select Duplicate. You'll now have the whole block attached to your pointer. Drag it down to the

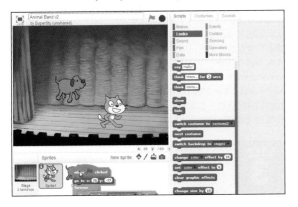

Sprites area, move the pointer over the dog and click. Now go back to the Scripts area, right-click on the extra block of script and select Delete.

STEP 14 The script you had attached to your cat is now attached to your dog, but we don't want him to appear in exactly the same place or play exactly the same notes through the same instrument. That means we need to adjust the values – the numbers – in the script. Click on the dog sprite, then go to the Scripts area and change the x: and y:

values in the 'go to' block to -70 and -80. Just click on the numbers and type in new numbers.

STEP 15 Now try setting the instrument in the set instrument block to 19, the marimba, then change the four notes to 48, 50, 52 and 53. Our canine chum now plays a cheerful upward scale all of his own.

STEP 16 Now, keep adding sprites until your band is assembled and ready to play. You can keep duplicating and dragging the same script from one to the next, remembering each time to add a new starter position, a new instrument and a new set of notes to play. Within minutes, your animal band will be up on stage and ready to perform. ●

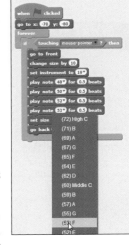

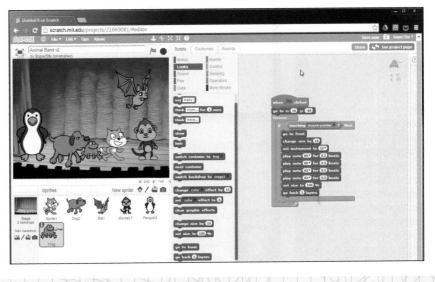

Animate a Scratch cartoon

Now you know some of the basics, you're ready for something more ambitious. How about a short scratch-powered cartoon?

Scratch is perfect for creating animations, as it has a library of characters, backdrops and sounds built in, and all the script blocks you need to make use of them. To see how it can be done, we're going to create a simple cartoon, but you can use the techniques you learn here to make something longer and even more exciting.

STEP 1 First, we need to get our sprites and backdrops ready. Click on the 'Choose backdrop from library' button, select the Castle4 backdrop and click OK. Next, right-click on the cat sprite in the Sprites area and select Delete. Now, using the 'Choose sprite from library'

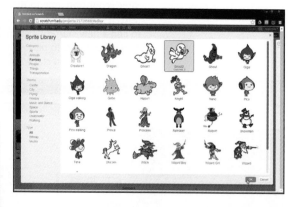

button, go and grab the Dog2 sprite, then the Ghost2 sprite. You can find them faster by clicking on the Animals and Fantasy categories on the left-hand side of the Sprite Library window.

STEP 2 Click on the Dog2 sprite in the Sprites area, and let's get scripting. Click on the Events category and drag the 'when green flag clicked' block into the Scripts area, then click

on the Motion category and drag in the 'point in direction x' block and the 'go to x:x y:y' block. Keep the first block as it is, but in the second set x to

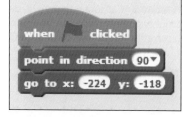

-224 and y to -118. This makes sure our dog is facing the right direction – it becomes important later – and puts him in exactly the right spot.

STEP 3 Here's how we animate him. Click on the Control category, then drag a 'repeat x' block into the Scripts area. Don't attach it to our stack right away. Now go to the Motion category, and drag the 'move x steps' block into the C shape of the 'repeat' block. To control the speed of the animation, we'll use a sound. Go to the Sounds category, and pull in the 'play drum x for y beats' block. Set the drum sound to 10 and the beats to 0.2.

Finally, go to Looks, and drag in the 'switch costume to x' block. Set the costume to dog2-b.

STEP 4 That sorts out one step of this two-step walk. For the next step, simply repeat the sequence of 'move x steps', 'play drum' and 'switch costume to x' blocks, then make some changes. Set the drum sound to 13 and the beats to 0.2,

ANIMATION

To animate a character, you need to use a sprite with more than one costume, where each costume can represent a frame of animation. With our dog, for example, each costume has the legs in different positions, which means that swapping from one costume to another will make it look like the dog is walking. The more costumes you have for a walking animation, the smoother and more realistic the animation will look. The old video games that used sprites sometimes used hundreds of frames just for one character's walks, runs and jumps!

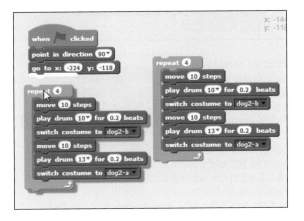

and switch the costume back to dog2-a. Finally, set the value of the 'repeat' block – the number of times it will repeat – to 4. That's our doggy animation block done, but don't attach it to the main script block, as we'll need it several times. Instead, right-click on it and duplicate it, then attach that version.

STEP 5
It's time to give our canine star the creeps. First, we'll add a noise. Click the Sounds tab, then click the 'Choose sound from library' button – it's the first one on the left under New Sound in the top-left corner. Click on the Effects category, select the 'door creak' sound, and press OK. Now, click the Scripts tab, and drag the Play sound x until done block into the Scripts area and start a new stack with it. Make sure the sound is set to the door creak.

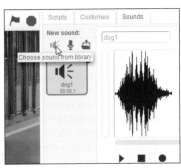

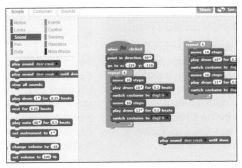

STEP 6
Click on the Looks category, drag in the 'Switch costume to x' block, and set the costume to 'dog2-c'. Click on the Control category, and drag in the 'wait x secs' block. Leave it set to 1. Pull in another 'switch costume to x' block, and set it to switch costume to 'dog2-a'. Finally, drag in a 'think x for x secs' block from Looks, and change the "Hmmm...." To "I'm not scared of ghosts...." and the time to 1 second.

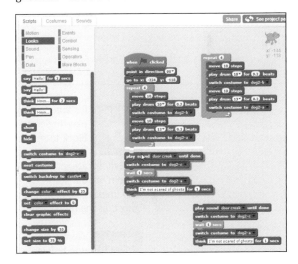

STEP 7
Again, we'll want to use this block more than once, so duplicate it, then drag the duplicate into place at the bottom of your main script. Give it a quick runthrough by clicking the script or pressing the green flag button at the top of the Stage area.

STEP 8
Now for the clever bit. We can save ourselves some work by reusing the two stacks we've made. Duplicate the animation stack again and drag it to the bottom of our main stack. Then duplicate the second stack – the one

that ends with 'I'm not scared of ghosts…' – and drag that below it. To add a little variety, click on the Sounds tab, add a second sound, Spooky String from the Instruments category, just like we did in step 5. Change the sound in the second 'I'm not scared…' block to the Spooky String sound.

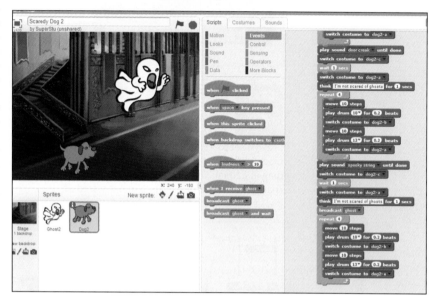

STEP 9 It's time to bring our second character into play. In Scratch, you can use the Broadcast block to send a message to another sprite, so that they can do something in return. Go to the Events category, and drag the 'broadcast' block to the bottom of your stack. Click the arrow next to the box with 'message1' in it, and select 'new message…' Type in 'ghost' as the message name and click OK.

STEP 10 We want our dog to keep on walking, so duplicate and drag the animation stack to the bottom of the main stack. Now click on the ghost in the Sprites area.

First, we need to set up a simple script to get him in the right position. Drag in the 'when green flag clicked' block, then the 'go to x: x y: y' block. Set x to 161 and y to -64. Drag in the 'set rotation style' block and set it to 'left-right', then the 'point in direction x' block. Set the direction to -90. Finally, go to the Looks category and drag in a 'hide' block. We don't want our ghost to be visible at first.

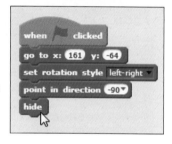

STEP 11 Now we need to decide what the ghost does when he gets the message. Go to the Events category, and drag in the 'when I receive' block to start a new stack. It should already

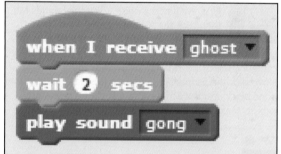

be set to 'ghost'. For the sake of suspense, go to the Control category and add a 'wait x secs' block, setting the value to 2. When our ghost appears, we want a shock, so add a new sound, just as we did before. This time we want the gong, which you can find in the Percussion category. Once you've added it, click on Scripts, then the Sound category, then drag in the 'play sound' block and set it to 'gong'.

CONTROL FLOW

In programming, the control flow is the order in which the individual statements or instructions in a program will run, and control flow statements are instructions which affect that order. We've already used the loop, which tells the program to run the same instructions again and again, either forever or a certain number of times. The If x then x block is another control flow statement, as it tells the program to do one thing if a certain thing is happening, or not. The Broadcast and When I receive blocks used here are more examples, as they tell one sprite to send a message that triggers an action from the other sprite. The When I receive block then defines what that action is.

STEP 12 A simple script makes our ghost appear. Go to the Looks category, and drag in the 'set x effect to x' block. Set the effect to 'ghost' and type in 250 as the value. Now drag in the 'show' block underneath. The ghost effect tells our scary spirit to remain invisible. Next, go to Control and drag in a 'repeat' loop. Return to the Looks category, and drag the 'change x effect by x' block. Set the loop to repeat 50 times, and set the effect to 'ghost' and the value to -5. This will make our ghost appear in spooky style.

STEP 13 That should scare our canine hero, so how will he react? Again, we can use the 'broadcast' block to find out. Go to the events category and drag a 'broadcast' block

to the bottom of the stack. As in step 9, select a new message and this time call it 'scare'. Now, click on the dog sprite so we can define how he takes his shock.

STEP 14 Drag the 'when I receive' block from the Events category into the Scripts area to start a new stack. Set the message to 'scare'. First, our dog will scream, then jump in fear. Add a new sound – screech from the Electronic category – then

click on the Scripts tab, then the Sound category. Drag in the 'play sound' block and set the sound to 'screech'.

STEP 15 For the jump, go to the Motion category and drag in the 'change y by x' block. Set the value to 20. Next, go to the Looks category, drag in a 'switch costume to x' block from the Looks category, and set the costume to 'dog-2c'. Now go to the Control category and drag in a 'wait' block, and type in 0.5 to set the value. Finally, go back to the Motion category, pull in another 'change y by x' block, and set the value to -20. Go to Looks, drag in a second 'switch costume to x' block, and set the costume back to 'dog2-a'.

STEP 16 Finally, let's have our dog turn tail and run away. Go to Motion, drag in a 'set rotations style' block and set it to 'left-right'. Next, grab the 'point in direction' block and set it to -90. Now we can reuse the animation block we set up earlier. Drag it into place at the bottom, then set the repeat value to 20, and the beats value for the two 'play drum' blocks to 0.02. This makes our dog run a faster, and sends him speeding home to end our short cartoon. ●

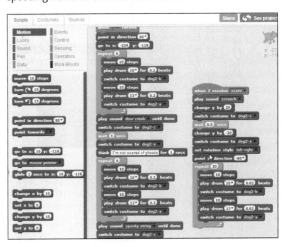

When crabs collide

When these crustaceans come together, you're guaranteed an explosive time!

I n the last two projects, we've started working with conditional statements. These are statements that tell the program to go one way or another, depending on whether a certain condition is met. The 'if x then x' block is the best example. Say you're in a car waiting at traffic lights. If the light is green, your car can go. If it's red or amber, you have to wait. Conditional statements work in exactly the same way.

We're going to use more conditional statements in this next project, as well as use a handy method of making many sprites from one, and play with some more motion blocks, sounds and visual effects. It's time to find out what happens when crabs collide...

STEP 1
As usual, there's a little preparation to start off with. Start a new project, then immediately right-click on the Scratch cat in the Sprites area and select Delete to get rid of it. Next, go to the Stage area, and click the 'Choose backdrop from library' button. Find 'underwater 1' in the Underwater category, click on it and press OK. Now go back to the Sprites area, and click on the 'Choose sprite from library' button. Select the Crab, and click OK.

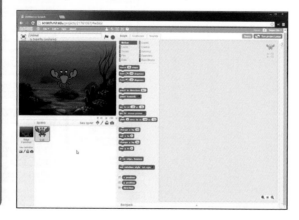

STEP 2
Let's give this crab its first script. Go to the Events category and drag out the good old 'when green flag clicked' block. Next, go to Looks and drag in the 'hide' block. Follow that with the 'set x effect to x block', then the 'set size to x %' block. Keep the effect set to 'color' but change the value to 120, then set the size to 33%. This makes a smaller blue crab, which you won't actually see, but will work as a kind of 'master crab' that we can use to make more crabs. It all comes down to the magic of cloning.

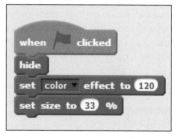

STEP 3
To clone our crab, we're going to start a second stack. Go to the Events category, and drag the 'when space key pressed' block to the Scripts area. Click the arrow next to 'space', and change the key to the 'up arrow'. Now go to the Sound category, and drag the 'play sound pop' block into position underneath. Finally, go the Control category, and pull the 'create clone of myself' block into place. Leave it set to 'myself'. This stack will look for users pressing the up arrow key, and make a nice pop sound and spawn new crabs every time it's pressed.

```
when [flag] clicked
hide
set color effect to 120
set size to 33 %

when up arrow key pressed
play sound pop
create clone of myself

when I start as a clone
go to x: -19 y: -32
```

STEP 4
The next stack will tell our cloned crabs how to behave once they've been spawned. Kick it off by going back to the Control category, and dragging the 'when I start as a clone' block into the Scripts area. Now, we don't want our crabs to always appear in the same area, but in a different place each time. Go to Motion, and drag a 'go to x: x y: y' block into place beneath the last block.

STEP 5
Now click on the Operators category. These are blocks that work on words or numbers and calculate results. Other blocks can then use these results, either showing them, using

```
when [flag] clicked
hide
set color effect to 120
set size to 33 %

when up arrow key pressed
play sound pop
create clone of myself

when I start as a clone
go to x: pick random 1 to 10 y: pick random 1 to 10
```

them for further calculations, or using them to decide what the program does next. Here we're looking for the 'pick random' block. This thinks of a random number between the two numbers that you give it, then tells the program what it is. Drag one of these blocks into the space for the x: coordinate of the 'go to...' block, then another into the space for the y: coordinate.

STEP 6
Stage coordinates can go anywhere from -240 to 240 in both the horizontal (left to right) and vertical (up and down) directions. All you need to do to make your clone appear anywhere, then, is enter -240 to 240 in both of the 'pick random' blocks. Now go to the Looks category

```
when [flag] clicked
hide
set color effect to 120
set size to 33 %

when up arrow key pressed
play sound pop
create clone of myself

when I start as a clone
go to x: pick random -240 to 240 y: pick random -240 to 240
show
```

and drag in a 'show' block, then press the green flag above the Stage to run the script. Try pressing the up arrow key to see where the clones appear. You might also spot that more clones appear with each press.

STEP 7
Now let's get our crabs moving along. Again, we're going to use a random number so they don't all move in the same direction. Go to the Motion category, and drag the 'point in direction' block into place. Now go back to the

```
when [flag] clicked
hide
set color effect to 120
set size to 33 %

when up arrow key pressed
play sound pop
create clone of myself

when I start as a clone
go to x: pick random -240 to 240 y: pick random -240 to 240
show
point in direction pick random 1 to 360
repeat 180
```

x: -19
y: -32

Operators, and drag the 'pick random x to x' block and drop it where the value should be for the 'point in direction' block. Set the start and end numbers to 1 and 360. Finally, grab a 'repeat' block from the Control category, and move this into place at the bottom of the stack. Set the 'repeat' value to 180.

STEP 8 We also need some script to move and animate our crab, a bit like the dog in our last project. In order, we need a 'move x steps' block, then a 'switch costume to x' block, then a 'wait x secs' block. You probably know where to find these by now. Set the number of steps to 5, set the costume to 'crab-b', and put the wait at just 0.05 secs. Now repeat the same three blocks, but this time set the costume to 'crab-a'. Finally, go to the Motion category, and drag in the 'if on edge, bounce' block. Once you've built it, drop the whole stack in the C shape of the 'repeat' block. Try the program out. You can watch the crabs drifting around.

STEP 9 I know what you're saying: didn't we promise you colliding crabs? Let's take care of that right now. Right-click on the Crab sprite in the Sprites area, and select Duplicate to copy the sprite. We now have a copy of our original crab, with all the scripts already in place. We need to tell our new

crabs apart, so move up to the first 'when green flag clicked' stack, and set the colour effect to 60. Now go down to the 'when up arrow key pressed' stack, and change the key to the down arrow.

STEP 10 We've now got lots of blue and green crabs, and we can keep on making new ones just by pressing the up and down arrow keys. Just run the script and give it a try! What we want, though, is for something interesting to happen when the two types collide. How about we make our new green crabs explosive, and our blue crabs react to

IF, THEN, ELSE

The 'if, then, else' block is a slightly more complex version of the 'f, then' conditional statement. It tells the program to check whether a condition has been met (like a green crab touching a blue crab), then what to do if it has. If it hasn't though, the 'else' part kicks in, and tells the program to keep doing something else. If you put the 'if, then, else' block in a 'repeat' or 'forever' block, it will keep on checking whether the condition has been met. Otherwise, it just checks once.

the blast? For this, we need some new script. Go to the Control category, and drag the 'if then else' block into the Scripts area. It looks like a letter E.

STEP 11 Go to the Sensing category, and drag the 'touching?' block into the space between the 'if' and 'then'. Click the arrow, and select 'Crab' from the list. This tells the program to watch out for green crabs hitting blue crabs. Now we need a sound to go with it. Click on the Sounds tab, then the 'Choose sound from library' button. This time' we want the zoop sound in the Electronic category. Once you have it, click on the Scripts tab, then the Sound category. Drag the 'play sound' block and drop it into the space between the top lines of the 'If then else' block's E.

STEP 12

Next, we need a simple explosion animation. Go to the Control category, and drag a 'repeat' block into position beneath that last 'play sound' block. Inside this, put a 'change x effect by x' block, then another 'wait' block. Set the effect to 'pixelate' and the value to 5, then set the wait to 0.02 secs. Finally, go to the Control category, and grab the 'delete this clone' block. Slot it into place underneath the 'repeat' block.

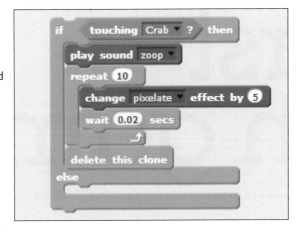

STEP 13

To get it all working, we need to move our blocks around. Click and drag the 'move 5 steps' block from its space inside the 'repeat' block – the stack below it will come with it – and put the whole lot in the space at the bottom of the 'if then else' block. Now drag the 'if then else' block, with everything in it, and slot that into the C shape of the 'repeat' block. Our new stack tells the program to look to see whether (the 'if' bit) a clone of this Crab2 sprite is touching a clone of the Crab sprite, and if so (the 'then' bit) run our pixelate animation and disappear. Otherwise (the 'else' bit), the script can just keep doing what it's doing, and keep our crab walking around.

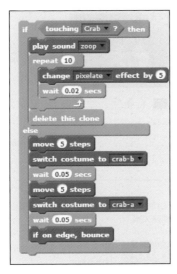

STEP 14

We want a different result for our other crab, but we can still save time by reusing the same blocks. Right-click on the 'repeat' block in the 'when I start as a clone' stack and select Duplicate. Now drag the duplicate block over to the Crab sprite in the Sprites area, and click the sprite to copy it there. Click on the Crab sprite, and you should see it. Right-click on the 'repeat' block attached to the existing stack to delete it and everything below, then drag the copied stack into position.

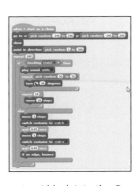

STEP 15

Now we need to make some changes. Click on the Sounds tab and add a new sound. Now change the 'touching?' block in the 'if, then' block to read 'Crab2', and change the sound in the 'play sound' block to 'rattle'. Now right-click on the 'repeat' block underneath and delete it. We're going to change this part of the stack completely.

STEP 16

Drag two more 'repeat' blocks into the Scripts area and stack them on their own. Go to the Operators and drag another 'pick random...' block into the top 'repeat' block, and set the values to 10 to 20. Underneath, pull in a 'turn x degrees' block from the Motion category and set it to 36 degrees. Now, drag a 'move x steps' block into the C shape of the second 'repeat' block, and set it to 5. Finally, drag it all into the 'repeat' block you emptied in step 9. ●

Your first Scratch game

It's time to take your Scratch skills up a notch or two by learning how to code this simple arcade shoot-em-up game

B
y now, you should be ready to tackle something bigger, so we're going to build our first Scratch game. Old-school arcade games are a good programming exercise. They involve a lot of interaction, we all know what the rules are and it's fairly easy to piece together how they should work. What's more, you get something you might want to play. This one is going to be a shoot-em-up, where marauding invaders turn up at the top of the screen and make their way down, while a spaceship at the bottom of the screen tries to dodge them or riddle them with bullets.

Before we start coding, let's think about what we need. Item one is the spaceship, which needs to move left and right, and fire bullets. Item two would be our invaders, and they need to appear at the top of the screen and move downwards towards the bottom. Item three would be the player's bullets, which need to travel upwards from the spaceship towards the invaders. That means we need to work with at least three sprites.

On top of this, we need to plan for three possible interactions. First, if a starfish invader hits the spaceship, the spaceship explodes and it's game over. Second, if the player fires the spaceship's cannons, a bullet needs to be released and travel up the screen. Finally, if a bullet hits a starfish, the starfish has to explode and the player's score has to go up. Now we know the basic elements, we can get them all working in the game.

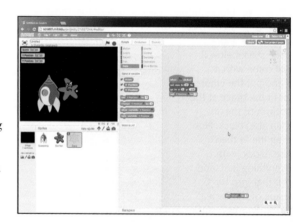

library' button, find and select them in the library, then click OK.

STEP 1
First, we need to get our most basic elements together. Right-click on the Scratch cat sprite to delete it, then go to the backdrop area, click the 'Choose backdrop from library' button, then select the Stars backdrop. Now, we need to get hold of our three sprites: the Spaceship, the Starfish and Star2. For all three, click the 'Choose sprite from

STEP 2
Click on the spaceship, and let's get scripting. The basic stack is pretty simple. First, we need the 'when green flag clicked' block, then we get a 'set size to x' block from the Looks category, and set the size to 25%. This makes our spacecraft a more manageable size. Now we drag in a 'go to x: x y: y' block from the Motion category, and set x to 0 and y to -120. This tells the spaceship to start at the bottom of the Stage.

STEP 3
We're going to use some variables to control the score and where our sprites and any clones appear on the screen. Click on the Data category, then click the Make a Variable button. Call the first variable 'Score' and click on the little

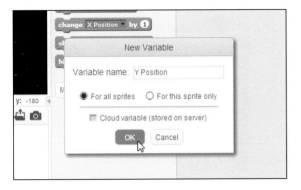

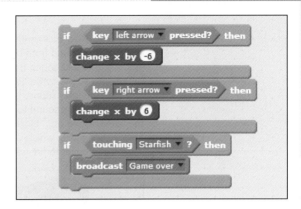

round radio button to make it available 'For all sprites'. Now repeat this step twice more, creating one variable called X Position and one variable called Y Position. Now drag the 'set variable to x' block into the Scripts area and place it at the bottom of the stack. Set the variable to 'Score' and leave the value at 0.

STEP 4
Now to control the spaceship's movement. Drag in a 'forever' block from Control and place it at the bottom of the stack. Next, drag an 'if then' block into the Scripts area and place it on its own. Go to the Sensing category, and drag the 'key x pressed?' block into the space at the top of the 'f then' block. Now go to Motion and pull in the 'change

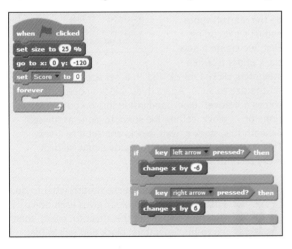

x by x' block. Set the key to the 'left arrow', and ask x to change by -6. Now duplicate this little block, and set the key to the 'right arrow', and ask x to change by 6. Stack the two blocks together. The first 'if' block tells the spaceship to move 6 pixels to the left if you press the left arrow, while the second tells it to move 6 pixels to the right when you press the right arrow.

STEP 5
Drag in another 'if then' block. This time, we need the 'touching?' block from the Sensing category, and a 'broadcast message' block from Control. Set the 'touching?' block to look for the Starfish sprite, and set up a new message,

which we'll call 'Game over'. Attach this block to the other two 'if then' blocks, then drag the whole stack inside the C shape of the 'forever' block.

STEP 6
We need three more blocks to finish this script. The first, 'if on edge, bounce' from the Motion category, tells our spaceship to bounce off if it hits the left- or right-hand edge of the screen. The other two set the two variables we set up earlier. Go to the Data category, and drag the 'set variable to x' block in twice, making sure each goes inside the 'forever' block. Set the first to X Position and the bottom to Y Position, but for the values go to the Motion category and drag in the 'X Position block' for the first, and the 'Y Position' block for the second. You'll find both at the bottom of the Blocks Palette. These variables will store the current location of the spaceship.

STEP 7
That's it for now for the spaceship; let's start work on the bullet. Click on the Star2 sprite and start a new stack with the 'when green flag clicked' block. Bring in a 'set size to x%' block and set it to 20, then a 'hide' block. Next, we need a 'forever' block, and inside that place an 'if then' block. Grab the 'key x pressed' block and drop it into place, and set the key to 'space'.

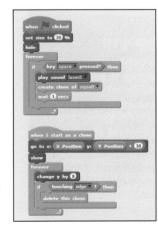

STEP 8 Now click on the Sound tab, then the 'choose a sound from library' button, and add the laser2 sound from the Electronic category to this sprite. Return to the Scripts menu, and drag the 'play sound' block into the 'if then' block, before setting the sound to 'laser2'. Beneath it, stack the 'create clone of...' block and set it to 'myself', then a 'wait x secs' block, which you should set to 1. This little stack tells a bullet to fire when the space key is pressed,

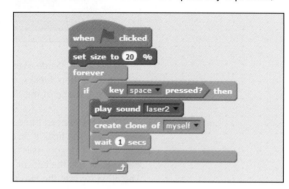

which actually means making the laser2 sound and creating a clone of the sprite. The 'wait' block limits the rate of fire.

STEP 9 This next script tells the cloned sprite where to appear and what to do. It starts off with a 'when I start as a clone' block, then it's time to use our variables. Pull out a 'go to x: y:' block from the Motion category, then go to Data and drag the block for the X Position variable into the space next to the x:. Now go to the Operators category and drag out the block at the top with two circular spaces separated by a plus. Drop it next to the y:. Now go back to Data and drag the 'Y position' block into the first circular space, then click in the second circular space and type 20. This tells our little bullet to appear wherever the spaceship is, but just above it.

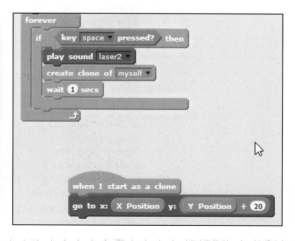

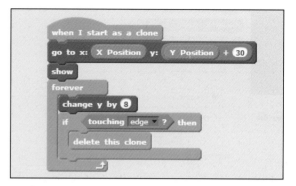

STEP 10 Next, stack the 'show' block, then a 'forever' block. Inside it, add a 'change y by...', block from the Motion category, and set the value to 8. Beneath that, add an 'if then' block. Grab another 'touching?' block from Sensing, and set it to 'edge'. Now get a 'delete this clone' block from Control, and drag it inside the 'if then' block.

STEP 11 We have a spaceship that moves and a bullet that it can fire upwards. All we need now is an enemy to shoot at. Click on the Starfish sprite and let's get coding. First, we create a new stack under a 'when green flag clicked' block. Pull in a 'set size to...' block and set the size to 33%. Add a 'hide' block underneath. Next comes a 'forever' block, and inside this we put a 'create clone of...' block, setting the sprite to clone as 'myself'. Beneath this, stack a 'wait' block, and set it to 1 secs. This stack tells the program to create a new starfish every second.

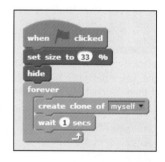

STEP 12 This next stack tells these starfish what to do. First, a 'set x effect' block gives each one a different colour. Set the effect to 'color', then go to the 'operators' block and pull in the 'pick random' block. Enter 1 and 200 as the values. Next,

we want a 'show' block, to make each Starfish appear. However, we want each to appear in a different place. Drag the 'go to x: y:' block into place at the bottom of the stack, and pull another 'pick random' block in next to the x:. Set the values in the 'random' block to -200 and 200, then set the y value in the 'go to' block to 148. This tells each starfish clone to pop up anywhere at the top of the screen, with a little space so that they don't appear right at the sides.

 STEP 13 This is where things get a bit complicated. We want out starfish to keep travelling downwards, unless it gets hit by a bullet or hits the bottom of the screen. The secret is to use two 'if, then, else' blocks, with one actually nested inside the other. Drag a 'forever' block to the bottom of the stack, then put the first 'if, then, else' block inside it. Next to the 'if', put a 'touching ?' block from the Sensing category, and set it to 'Star2'. Inside this block, drag the

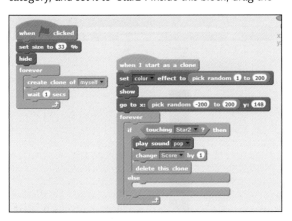

'play sound' block with it set to 'pop', then go to the 'data' block and find the 'change variable to x' block. Change the variable to 'Score' and set it to change by 1. Finally, pull a 'delete this clone' block into place. If a bullet hits a Starfish, it will make a pop noise, increase the score by 1, then disappear.

STEP 14 Now drag a second 'if, then, else' block inside the bottom space of the first. This time, pull a 'touching?' block into place next to the 'if' and set it to 'edge'. Go to the Control category, and pull a 'delete this clone' block into the space underneath. If a starfish hits the bottom edge of the screen, it will now disappear.

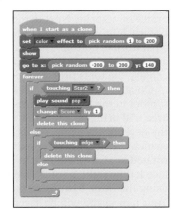

ABOUT VARIABLES

Variables are a common element of any programming language. They work like the values that we type into a block of script to tell a sprite to go to a specific point or a 'repeat' block to repeat ten times. But with a variable, the number is stored elsewhere by the program, and retrieved every time a block asks for it. In effect, the number gets stored in a box with a label. We tell the program what to store in the box, and it only has to ask for the label to use whatever number is in it.

This has a lot of advantages. First, you can share a variable between different parts of the program. For example, you could use a variable to track the horizontal position of one sprite so that the program knows when another sprite is directly above it. We'll use this with the 'X Position' block when we want our spaceship to fire bullets. We can also change and make calculations with variables. We could control the size of a series of oranges by defining a variable called size, then making the number a little bit bigger with every orange. The more complex your program is, the more you'll want to use variables, and the more useful they become.

STEP 15 All we need to do now is get our starfish moving. Just get a 'change y by…' block from the Motion category and drag it into the space underneath the bottom X. Set the value to -2.

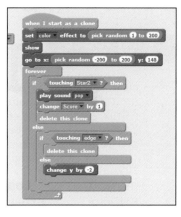

STEP 16 Finally, we need to sort out what happens when our spaceship gets hit by a falling starfish. Remember the 'Game over' message we set to broadcast earlier? Create a new stack on any of the sprites with a 'when I receive message' block. Set the message to 'Game over'. Drag in a 'say x for x secs' block, and set it to say GAME OVER for two seconds. Then go to the Control category, and grab a 'stop' block. Leave it set to 'all'. If your ship is now hit by a starfish, the game will stop. Not very exciting, we know. If only there was something we could do… ●

Remix the game

Not satisfied with your finished game? The great thing about programming is that you can go back and fix it, or even make it more spectacular!

T alk to any programmer and they'll tell you that few projects are ever really finished – there's always something you can do to improve them. With this in mind, we're going to take another look at our first Scratch game. It's functional and playable as it is, but what would it be like if we changed the graphics and added music, or made it a little more exciting? It's time to find out.

Load up the game
You can load any project you've already created by clicking on the My Stuff folder in between the Messages icon and Your profile icon on the Scratch web page. You'll see all your existing projects listed. Alternatively, you can click on the File menu in any open Scratch project, then select Go to My Stuff. Open a project from the list by clicking on it, then click the See Inside button to go back, edit and remix it.

▲ Click on Go to My Stuff on the File menu in any open Scratch project to see all your existing projects listed.

▲ You can load any project you've already created by clicking on the My Stuff folder.

Transform your spaceship
There's nothing wrong with Scratch's built-in spaceship, but was it really built for a fast-paced action game? No. If you want to change the way it looks, you have two options. The first is to create a brand-new sprite. Next to the 'Choose sprite from library' button at the top of the Sprites area there's a paintbrush button: 'Paint new sprite'. Click this and you'll bring up the Costumes Editor, where you can use the tools provided to draw a new sprite.

Once you've finished, clicking on the blue 'i' symbol in the top left of the sprite in the Sprites area will bring up a window where you can type the new sprites name, set its starting direction (which way it faces) and set whether it can be rotated so that it will face in any direction, only face left or right, or only face in one direction, using the three buttons marked rotation style. Your new sprite will be saved when you next save your project. The only downside of this approach is that you'll need to copy all the scripts for the on it in the Sprites area, then click the Costumes tab above the Blocks Palette. Click the 'Paint new costume' button above the two existing costumes, and start drawing. When you're finished, you can just delete the old costumes by clicking on them in the list, then clicking the x on the right-hand side of the highlight box. Alternatively, you can just ensure your sprite is highlighted in the list of costumes, then add a 'Switch costume to x instruction at the start of the Sprite script, and set it to the new costume.

Add some animation

We can make our starfish even more fearsome by adding a little animation to the Sprite. All it takes are a few additions to the Starfish script. Click on the Starfish sprite in the Sprites area, then on the

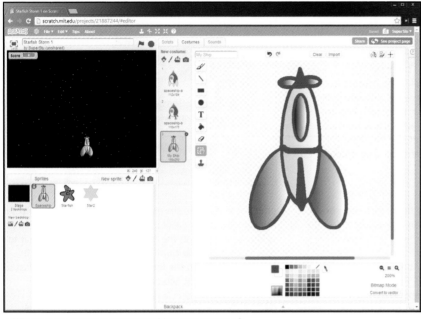

▲ Why not give your exisiting spaceship a new costume?

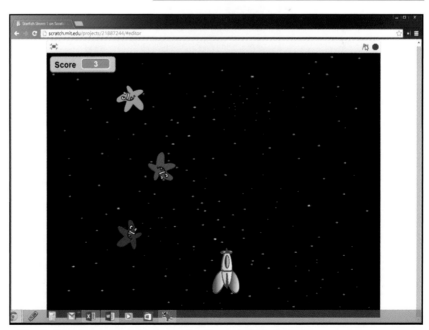

old spaceship over to the new one, and change any references made to the spaceship to the new sprite's name.

The alternative? You can give your existing Spaceship sprite a new costume. Simply click

▲ The starfish now turn around and around as they make their descent.

33

Scripts tab to edit its scripts. We need to adjust its default behaviour – what the sprite does when it isn't being touched by a bullet, and it hasn't touched the edge of the screen. See where the block says 'change y by -2'? That's it.

We're not going to use different frames of animation this time. We just want our starfish to turn around and around as they fall. We do this by adding a 'turn x degrees' block below the 'change y by -2' block, and set the rotation to '5'. Our starfish now turn smoothly as they make their menacing descent.

Make a new enemy

Our starfish put up a decent fight, but any good arcade game needs more than one enemy, so you might want to add this killer super-starfish.

STEP 1 You can start off by duplicating the original starfish. Click in the 'I' in the top left of the highlight box that appears when he's selected if you want to change his name. Here, we're calling him SuperStar. It's once you get to the scripts, however, that you need to make some changes. First, take a look at the 'when Green flag clicked' stack. This script is still designed to keep on producing clones, but here we've put in a 'pick random' block in the 'wait'

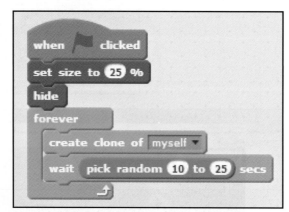

block instead of the usual 1 second value. This means a new super-starfish will now spawn at random intervals between 10 and 25 seconds, making him a more dangerous and unpredictable opponent. We've also changed the size of the sprite to just 25%, to make him smaller and harder to hit.

STEP 2 Look at the 'when I start as a clone' stack, and you'll see more changes. First, we've added a sound to the sprite: the space ripple from the Electronic category. If we place this here, before the 'forever' loop, this spooky sample will play every time a super-starfish appears. We've also created a new variable called 'colour', which we're using for a cool colour-change effect. We've added a 'set color

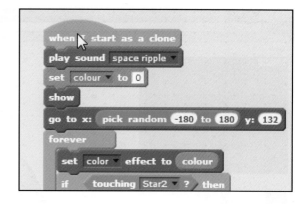

effect to x' block to the start of the 'forever' loop, and set the value to use the Colour variable. By putting a 'change colour by x' block at the end of the loop and setting it to 5, we can make the clone change colour every time its script runs through the loop, which happens pretty fast as he moves down the screen.

STEP 3 Finally, this enemy has a different style of movement. He mercilessly hunts down our player's spaceship. We do this by replacing the old 'change y by -2' block at the bottom of the second 'if, then, else' block so that it uses a 'point towards' block, set to the Spaceship sprite, then moves 4 steps towards that target. This tells the sprite to keep pointing at the spaceship, wherever it's moving, then move steadily towards it. Our spaceship will now have to shoot it to survive.

STEP 4 To make super-starfish a credible threat, we also need to change the spaceship's script. If you look, we've added a fourth 'if then' block to the stack, identical to the one that looks to see whether the spaceship is touching the original starfish.

```
        broadcast  Game over ▼

if        touching  SuperStar ▼  ?   then
        broadcast  Game over ▼

if on edge, bounce

set   X Position ▼  to   x position

set   Y Position ▼  to   y position
```

Set this to the SuperStar sprite, and it's game over if our spaceship makes contact with our super-starfish.

Making Game Over mean something

At the moment, the Game Over message is a bit of a damp squib. For a start, we could make our spaceship explode, using the same pixelate effect we used in our 'When Crabs Collide' project. Look at the new script, and you can see that we've changed the 'stop' block to read 'other scripts in sprite', then added the screech sound and a 'play sound' block to play it. We then run

```
when I receive  Game over ▼

stop   other scripts in sprite ▼

play sound  screech ▼

repeat  5
    change  pixelate ▼  effect by  10

say  Game Over  for  2  secs

say  You Scored  for  2  secs

say  Score  for  2  secs

stop  all ▼
```

◀ Have a go at making the Game Over message a bit more exciting.

▶ Even better, why not add some music in the form of the classic funeral march?

a short loop with a Pixelate effect that turns our spaceship into a pile of chunks. We then add three 'say' blocks, each one running for two seconds. The first says 'Game Over', the second says 'You Scored', and the third looks at the current value of the Score variable and reports the score. Add a 'stop all' instruction at the end, and it's a much better Game Over.

Music

Still, we could make it even better. This little stack adds the classic funeral march used by so many vintage arcade games. Just stick it in between the

```
set instrument to  20 ▼

play note  60 ▼  for  0.5  beats

wait  0.05  secs

play note  60 ▼  for  0.2  beats

wait  0.05  secs

play note  60 ▼  for  0.2  beats

wait  0.05  secs

play note  60 ▼  for  0.5  beats

wait  0.05  secs

play note  63 ▼  for  0.2  beats

wait  0.1  secs

play note  62 ▼  for  0.2  beats

wait  0.1  secs

play note  62 ▼  for  0.4  beats

wait  0.02  secs

play note  60 ▼  for  0.2  beats

wait  0.03  secs

play note  60 ▼  for  0.3  beats

wait  0.03  secs

play note  59 ▼  for  0.2  beats

wait  0.03  secs

play note  60 ▼  for  1  beats
```

Pixelate animation and the Game Over messages, and it should work pretty well.

Make some waves

Classic arcade games used to have aliens that came in waves, increasing the difficulty as the player goes on. How can we make this happen here? Using variables, of course.

STEP 1
We use one – wave count – to work out how many starfish the player has destroyed. When the count hits 20, the game starts the next wave. We then use another two – spawn rate and speed – to tell the program how quickly to spawn new starfish, and how fast to make them move.

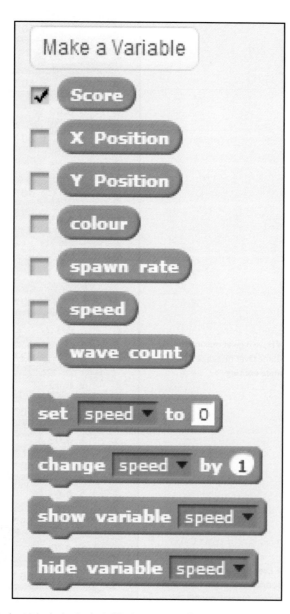

STEP 2
Once we've made our variables, we need to put them in a handful of scripts. First, go to the Starship script and add a 'set x to x' block from Data, setting it to wave count and 0.

STEP 3
Next, go to the Starfish sprite, and underneath the 'change score by 1' block put in an identical block reading 'change wave count by 1'. Underneath this, we add an 'if then' block from the Control category, with an 'x=x' block from the Operators. Drop the Wave Count variable into the first space, then type 20 in the second. In the space underneath, put in a 'broadcast message' block, with a new message called 'New Wave', then a new 'set

wave count' block to reset the Wave Count variable to 0. This tells the starfish to keep adding 1 to wave count every time a starfish is destroyed, and when the wave count hits 20, to broadcast a new wave message. Then it resets the wave count to 0.

STEP 4
Now what happens when the New Wave message is broadcast? Well, first we add a whole new block to the Spaceship sprite, which tells it to say 'New Wave Incoming!' when it gets the message. Second, we need to make a few more changes to both Starfish scripts. In the first

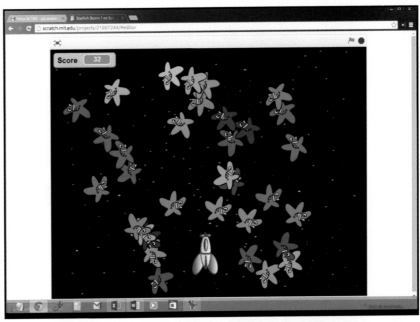

▲ Here's our improved game with its waves of starfish that increase in difficulty as the player goes on.

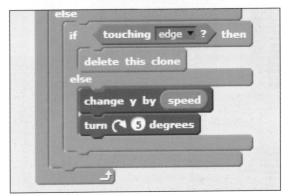

up when we have a new wave of starfish.

STEP 6
If we now go back to the 'when I receive New Wave' stack in the Spaceship sprite, we can set the Speed variable to change by -0.2, slightly increasing the speed our starfish move at. We can also add another block to change the spawn rate by -0.2, increasing the rate at which our starfish are spawned. The game will now get more difficult with each new wave. ●

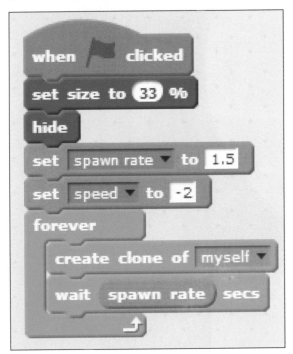

script, you can see we've added new 'set x to x' blocks from the Data category to set the spawn rate to 1.5 and the speed to -2. This tells the game to start off by releasing a new starfish every 1.5 secs, with the speed pretty slow. If we change the value in the 'wait' block to use the Spawn Rate variable, it will use this to decide how long to wait.

STEP 5
In the second script, we now need to change the 'change y by -2' block near the bottom to 'change y by the Speed variable'. This allows us to speed things

WHAT NEXT?

You can carry on enhancing the game if you want. Why not change backgrounds with each new wave, add a new intro music to the game, or add a high score chart? Don't worry if you don't know how to do these things right now. We'll be covering them in later projects.

Chapter

2

Section 2
Build your skills

By now, you've encountered many of the basic building blocks of computer science, and put them to good use in simple projects. Scratch's drag-and-drop approach is ideal for these first steps into coding, but it's capable of a lot more.

In this chapter, we're going to look at some more advanced Scratch programs, using variables, one-dimensional arrays, subroutines and more.

You'll discover how to do more with Scratch graphics, and how to create painting apps, racing games and other programs. Most importantly, all the knowledge you gain here will be relevant later on when we explore more complex ways to code.

Sounds difficult? It won't be. The more you learn about coding, the more logical it becomes, and before long you'll be prepared for what comes next.

Fun with Scratch graphics

Scratch can do a whole lot more than push spaceships and starfish around the screen. It's time to discover what other exciting features it has to offer

So far, we've used backgrounds, speech bubbles, thought bubbles and sprites to fill the screen, but Scratch also has another way of handling graphics: the pen. This is a really useful tool, which lets a sprite work as a pen, drawing on the screen as it moves. You can set whether the pen is drawing or not, and change the colour, shade and width of the line. What's more, you can control all these things – just like you would the sprite – using script blocks, and even use variables to alter the settings as the program runs.

Here, we're going to show how versatile the pen is by making a random pattern generator program, which takes a series of instructions, including a few random numbers, to create a whole range of fascinating, multicoloured patterns. And once we've got the random pattern generator working, we'll show you how to customise the program to give the user more control.

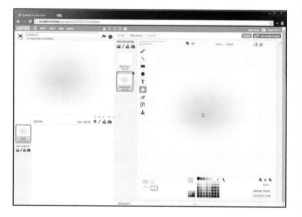

click the Paintbrush icon to 'Paint new backdrop'. Click the Paintpot tool to select 'Fill with color', then choose the round gradient fill from the group of four buttons, bottom left. Choose a nice light blue colour by clicking on it in the Colour Palette, then just click in the middle of the screen. Hey presto, one simple but attractive background.

STEP 1
If it's there, start by deleting the Scratch cat sprite. Now, our first job is to create a really simple background. Go down to the Backdrops area next to the Sprites area and

STEP 2
Next, we need an incredibly simple sprite. Go to the Sprites area and click the Paintbrush icon there to 'Paint new sprite'. Click the Brush to select it from the toolbar on the left, then choose a bright red colour from the Colour Palette. Move the line-width slider to the left of the Colour Palette to get a slightly thicker

line. Now, all you have to do is put a single, tiny dot right in the faint cross in the middle of the Painting area. Don't worry if you miss. You can either click the Clear button at the top and redo it, or the 'Set costume centre' button (the last of the three at the top right of the Costumes area) to move the cross. Either way works.

STEP 3 We've built our sprite. It's time to put it to work. This is another project where we can use clones to get a lot of work done very quickly, so we start off building a script to set

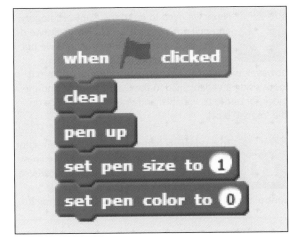

our master sprite up, then spawn them. First, pull in the 'when green flag clicked' block, then click on the Pen category. We need to reset the Stage and the status of the pen every time the program starts, so drag in a 'clear' block, then a 'pen up' block, then a 'set pen size to...' block and finally a 'set pen color to…' block.

STEP 4 Enter 2 as the value in the 'set pen size to' block, then go to the Operators category and drag a 'pick random x to x' block to the space in the 'set pen colour to' block. Set the values to 0 and 199. This will give us a random starting colour for each pattern we generate. Now go to the Motion

category and pull in a 'go to x: x y: y' block, then a 'point in direction' block. Set the x and y coordinates for the first block to 0 and 0, then drag in another 'pick random x to x' block and drop it on the space in the 'point in direction' block. Set the values to 1 and 360.

STEP 5 Our sprite will now start off each run in the middle of the Stage, with a random pen colour, ready to move off in a random direction. To control where it moves to next and to make sure it keeps on moving, we're going to use

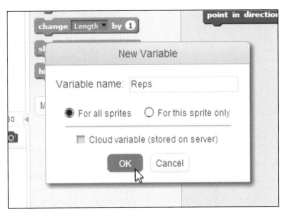

variables. Click on the Data category and make three new variables, which we'll call Angle, Length and Reps. You'll see three counters appear on the screen. Click the checkbox next to each variable if you want to switch its counter off or on again.

STEP 6 We now need to set the starting values for the first two variables. Drag in two 'set variable to x' blocks and stack them underneath the existing stack. Change the first to read 'Angle'

and 1, and the second to read 'Length' and 10. Now go to the Control category and pull in the 'create clone of' block, and make sure it's set to clone 'myself'. Finally, go to Looks and drag in a 'hide' block.

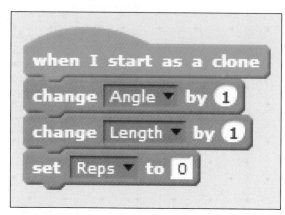

STEP 7
We now start a new stack with the 'when I start as a clone' block from Control. This block will control how the individual clones behave. To make an interesting pattern, we want each clone spawned to behave differently, so we pull in three blocks from the Data category to affect their behaviour. First, we need two 'change variable by x' blocks, then a 'set variable to x' block. Set the first block to 'Angle', the second to 'Length' and the third to 'Reps'.

STEP 8
We want each variable to change by a small amount each time, so that each clone does a slightly different thing. Go to Operators and drag in three 'pick random' blocks, placing each one carefully in the space where the value should go in our three data blocks. The Angle block needs to be set to -10 to 20. The Length block needs to be set to 10 to 40. Finally, the Reps block needs to be set to 10 to 80. When you're done, add the next block: 'pen down', from the Pen category.

STEP 9
Next, we need to go to the Control category and pull out a 'repeat' block. Normally, we'd set this block to loop the instructions we put inside it a set number of times. This time, however, we're going to control the number of times it loops using a variable. Go to the Data category, find the block for our Reps variable, and drag this into place on the 'repeat' block.

STEP 10
To produce its patterns, our pattern generator continuously changes the length of the lines it draws. If those lines get too long, however, you just end up with a dull pattern. We control the length using an 'if, then, else' block. Drag it

inside the C shape of the 'repeat' block, then go to the Operators and find the block that reads 'x > x'. This operator is looking to see whether the number on the left is larger than the number on the right.

STEP 11
Grab the block for the Length variable from Data, and drop it in the left-hand space. Now type 59 in the right-hand space. Next, drag the 'set variable to x' block out and drop it into the space underneath. Change the variable to Length, and change the value to 1. You're telling the

```
when I start as a clone
change Angle ▼ by pick random -10 to 20
change Length ▼ by pick random 10 to 40
set Reps ▼ to pick random 10 to 80
pen down
repeat Reps
    if  Length > 59  then
        set Length ▼ to 1
    else

```

CONTROLLING THE PEN

Scratch's pen lays down a line as the sprite it's attached to moves, and you can use the Pen blocks to control when the line is drawn or not, and also how it will look. Drag the 'pen down' block into a sprite, and the pen will draw a line from that point on. Drag the 'pen up' block into play, and the drawing stops. Three blocks control the pen's colour. The one with a block of colour at the end will set the pen to the currently selected colour, while the 'set pen colour to x' block, where x is a value or a variable, will set the pen to the colour associated with that number. The 'change pen colour' block can then adjust that number, moving the colour towards one end or the other of the colour spectrum. The 'set pen shade' and 'change pen shade' blocks set the pen to the brightest (highest) or lowest (darkest) shades of the colour, so that you'll get a bright blue line or a nearly black or white one, while the 'set pen size' and 'change pen size' blocks alter the width of the line to make it thinner or thicker.

program to look at the Length variable, see if it's over 59, and, if it is, to reset it back to 1.

STEP 12 If it's under 59, however, we want the program to increase Length by 1. Get the 'change variable by x' block and drag it into place in the space beneath the 'else'. Set the value to 1.

```
when I start as a clone
change Angle ▼ by pick random -10 to 20
change Length ▼ by pick random 10 to 40
set Reps ▼ to pick random 10 to 80
pen down
repeat Reps
    if  Length > 59  then
        set Length ▼ to 1
    else
        change Length ▼ by 1
    move 10 steps
    turn ↺ 15 degrees
```

block, which is the one with the arrow pointing to the left.

```
when I start as a clone
change Angle ▼ by pick random -10 to 20
change Length ▼ by pick random 10 to 40
set Reps ▼ to pick random 10 to 80
pen down
repeat Reps
    if  Length > 59  then
        set Length ▼ to 1
    else
        change Length ▼ by 1
```

STEP 13 Now it's time for the bit that tells each clone where it needs to draw. First, go to the Motion category, and drag a 'move x steps' block into the stack, making sure that it fits underneath the 'if, then, else' block, but above the bottom part of the 'repeat' block. Then, underneath it, place a 'turn anticlockwise x degrees'

```
when I start as a clone
change Angle ▼ by pick random -10 to 20
change Length ▼ by pick random 10 to 40
set Reps ▼ to pick random 10 to 80
pen down
repeat Reps
    if  Length > 59  then
        set Length ▼ to 1
    else
        change Length ▼ by 1
    move Length steps
    turn ↺ Angle degrees
```

STEP 14 We actually control these blocks using the variables we made earlier. Go to the Data category, and drag the Length variable, where the value should go in the 'move' block, and the Angle variable where the value should go in the 'turn' block. The program looks at the current Length, and moves that many steps in its current direction. It then looks at the current Angle, and changes its direction by that amount before moving on.

STEP 15

All that code will create just one line, so we need to keep creating clones to make more lines. Go to the Control category, and find the 'create clone of x' block. Drop it in place underneath the last two blocks, and make sure that it's set to 'myself'.

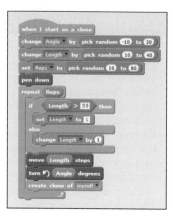

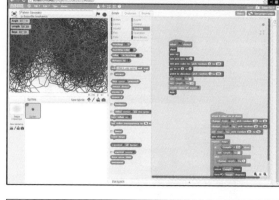

STEP 16

Now we need to make sure the line keeps changing colour. Go back to the Pens category, and find the 'change pen colour by x' block. Drag this in and drop it beneath the 'create clone' box, and you'll have a working pattern generator. Give it a spin!

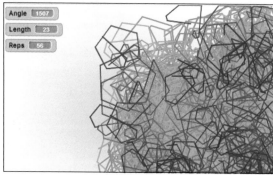

STEP 17

As it is, our pattern generator is working pretty well, but wouldn't it be great if we could influence how it works and the patterns it makes? We can. There are a couple of ways of doing it, but here we're going to use Scratch's 'ask and wait' block. To make it work, we're going to need to do a bit more scripting. First, go to the Sensing category and look for the 'ask and wait' block. By default, it has the question 'what's your name?'.

STEP 18

Drag it to the scripts area and into the 'when green flag clicked' stack, putting it just above the orange 'set Angle to 1' block. Change the text to read 'Enter Starting Angle'.

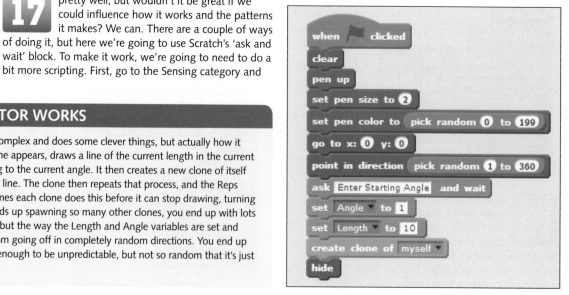

HOW THE GENERATOR WORKS

The pattern generator looks complex and does some clever things, but actually how it works is very simple. Each clone appears, draws a line of the current length in the current direction, then turns according to the current angle. It then creates a new clone of itself and changes the colour of the line. The clone then repeats that process, and the Reps variable decides how many times each clone does this before it can stop drawing, turning and cloning. As each clone ends up spawning so many other clones, you end up with lots of clones all drawing at once, but the way the Length and Angle variables are set and changed prevents the lines from going off in completely random directions. You end up with a pattern that's random enough to be unpredictable, but not so random that it's just a total mess.

OTHER IDEAS

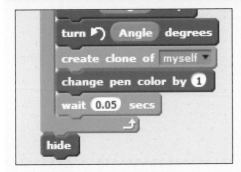

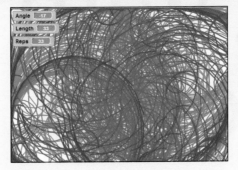

1 You can get a better idea of what the program is doing by adding a Show block to reveal the Cone sprites moving as they draw and adding a 'wait' block to the main 'repeat' loop to slow things down a little. Put a 'hide' at the bottom of the stack so you don't spoil the finished pattern. Give it a try!

2 You can also see what happens when the shade changes instead of the colour. Simply drag out the 'change pen colour by 1' block and replace it with a 'change pen shade colour by...' block, setting it to -1 to keep getting darker, or 1 to keep getting brighter.

3 You can also try messing about with the line width. To do it, we've created a new variable called Width, and set the pen size to use that variable in the 'when I start as a clone' stack. We then use an 'if, then, else' block, just like we did with the Length earlier, to control the maximum setting. Take a look at the stack, and see if you can work out how it works.

STEP 19 Now go back to the Blocks Palette and find the 'answer' block. Drag this to the 'set angle to' block, and drop it where you can currently see the 1. When the program runs from now on, it will ask the user to 'Enter Starting Angle'. When the user types this in and presses the Enter key, the program stores what they type as a kind of special variable – the Answer. By telling the 'set angle to' block to use the answer, we tell it to look at and use whatever's stored in Answer. Only one Answer can be stored this way at any time, so we need to use it before we can ask another question.

STEP 20 We could repeat these same three steps for the Length variable, but as this already has a limit set on it, the change wouldn't make much difference to the program or the pattern. Instead, it makes more sense to change the number of repetitions. Drag in a new 'ask and wait' block below the 'set angle to' block, and change the text to Enter Repetitions.

STEP 21 Now go to the second stack – the one that starts with 'when I start as a clone' – and find the block that reads 'set Reps to pick random 10 to 80'. Drag out the 'pick random' operator, and replace it with the 'answer' block. The number of repetitions won't be random anymore, giving the user more control over the pattern. While you're there, it's worth changing the values in 'change Angle by pick random to -5 and 5'. Again, this makes it easier to influence the finished pattern. Try running the program with different combinations of Angle and Repetitions to see what happens. ●

Paint with Scratch

In this project, we're going to push Scratch further than we ever have before by creating our very own Scratch painting program

Scratch gets used a lot to make games, quizzes and funny cartoon animations, but with a bit of thought it can be used to make almost any kind of program. We're going to prove that with this next project by building a simple painting program, complete with basic tools to paint lines, a choice of different colours, and even tools to stamp and paint with pictures on the page. It might sound like a lot of hard work, but with Scratch's built-in features it's easier than you'd think.

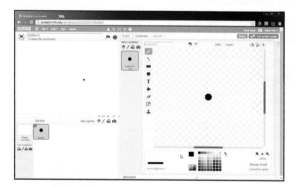

STEP 1
Start off by deleting the Cat sprite, then create a new Dot sprite, just like we did in the last project. Click the 'Paint new sprite' button at the top of the Sprites area. When the Costume Editor loads, increase the line width to the halfway mark, then stick a small blob of paint smack in the centre of the crosshairs. It helps if you press the magnifying glass to zoom into 400%.

STEP 2
That's our main sprite done, so click on the Scripts tab and let's get scripting. First, we're going to make our pointer work like a paintbrush. Our stack kicks off with the

'when green flag clicked' block. Then, go to the Pen category and drag out the 'clear' block. This clears the screen every time our paint program is run. Now go to Control, and drag a 'forever' block into place. If

you remember, this block tells the program to keep on doing whatever instructions we put inside it for as long as this stack is running.

STEP 3
Before we go on, we need to create some variables. We're going to use these to control the colour and shade of the paint our brush lays down, as well as the size of the brush. For each one, go to the Data category and click the Make a Variable button, then enter the name of the variable, and set it to work

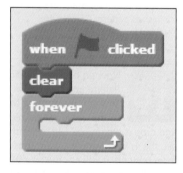

'For all sprites'. Call the three variables Colour, Shade and Size. You can leave the checkboxes next to Shade and Size ticked, but untick the one next to Colour.

 STEP 4 Go over to the Stage area, and right-click on the Shade counter. Select Slider from the dropdown menu that appears, and your Shade

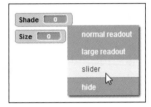

counter turns into a slider, where you can move the slider left and right to alter the value of the Shade variable. You can try it right now if you like, but the really cool thing is that anyone using the program will be able to do the same thing. Now drag the new Shade slider over to the top-right corner of the screen.

STEP 5 Do the exact same thing with the Size counter, then drag the new slider into place beneath the Shade slider. Now right-click again on the Shade slider, and select 'Set

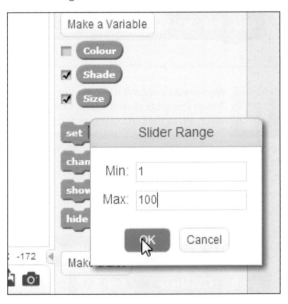

slider min and max' from the menu. Enter 1 as the minimum and 100 as the maximum. Do the same with the Size slider, and enter 1 as the minimum and 20 as the maximum.

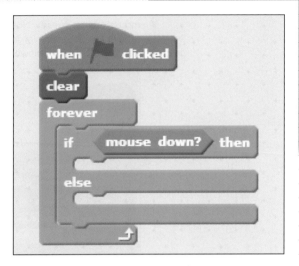

STEP 6 Right, let's get back to our script. Go to Control and find the 'if, then, else' block, and drag it into place inside the C shape of the 'forever' block. Now go to the Sensing category, find the 'mouse down?' block, and drag it into the space after the 'if'.

STEP 7 We've set this script to keep an eye on the mouse button, and see if it's being pressed or not. Now we need to tell it what to do if the mouse button is pressed. First, go to Motion, and drag in the 'go to x' block. It should be set to

47

mouse-pointer already. Now go to the Pen category, and drag in the 'set pen color to', 'set pen shade to' and 'set pen size to' blocks, followed by the 'pen down' block.

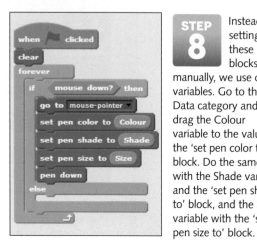

STEP 8 Instead of setting these blocks manually, we use our variables. Go to the Data category and drag the Colour variable to the value in the 'set pen color to' block. Do the same with the Shade variable and the 'set pen shade to' block, and the Size variable with the 'set pen size to' block.

STEP 9 When the mouse button is pressed, our sprite will now draw a line using our current settings for Shade, Size and Colour. And if it isn't, drag the 'pen up' block from the Pen category and place it inside the space underneath the 'else'. Give the script so far a try. You'll be able to draw a black line by clicking and holding the mouse button as you move the mouse around the screen. You can even change the width of the line by sliding the Size slider up and down.

STEP 10 It works, but wouldn't you like some colour? We can fix that by making a new sprite. Click the 'Paint new sprite' button and use the Rectangle tool to draw a small square over the crosshair. You can either fill it with the 'Fill with color' tool or click on the filled shape option in the bottom right of the Costume Editor. Remember, you can always use the Set Costume Centre tool later if you don't quite get it right.

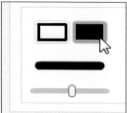

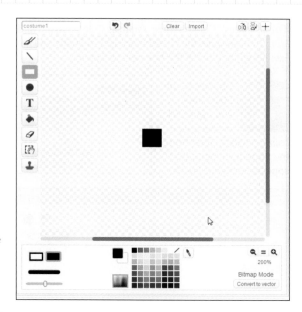

STEP 11 Click on the Scripts tab, and we can start scripting what this sprite will do. First, we need to reposition it, so grab a 'when green flag clicked' block, then attach a 'go to x: x y: y' block to it. Set x to -220 and y to 160.

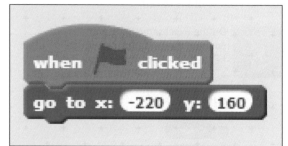

STEP 12 Now create a second stack, starting with a 'when this sprite clicked' block. Once that's in place, go to the Data category and pull in two 'set variable to x' blocks. Set the first one to 'Colour' and 0, and the second one to 'Shade' and 0. In effect, we've turned this sprite into a button. Click on it, and it turns the colour of the line to black.

STEP 13 That's great, but what about the colours? Well, we could keep making a new sprite for each colour and create a brand-new script for each, but why work when a little scripting will do the work for us? We can keep duplicating this sprite, and make a few changes for each version. Before we duplicate anything, look at the 'when Green flag clicked' sprite. Go to the Operators category and drag the 'x – x' block into the 'Go to x: x y: y' block, where the 160 is at the moment. Set the first value to 160 and the second to 0.

STEP 14 Now go to the Looks category and pull in the 'change x effect by x' block twice. Set the first one to 'color' and set the value to 0, and the second one to 'brightness' and the value

to 0. We don't actually want these two blocks to affect this sprite, but they make things a lot easier once we start duplicating it. Now right-click on the sprite in the Sprites area and select Duplicate.

STEP 15 Just click on the new Sprite to highlight it, then it's time to adjust the script. By changing the second value in the Operator block in the 'go to x: x y: y' block, you can quickly change the vertical position of the sprite. Setting it to 25 works well in our example. Now you need to change the colour

of the sprite, by changing the settings for the Color and the Brightness effects. Here, we want a red, so set the Color effect to change by 1, and the Brightness effect to change by 100.

STEP 16 Now we just need to go over to the 'when this sprite clicked' stack and set it up to match. Set the Color to 1, then set the Shade to 50. Now, when you run the script, the

bottom of our two black square sprites will now look red, and produce a red line when clicked.

STEP 17 The beauty of doing things this way is that you can keep on duplicating the last sprite, then change the values to alter its colour, and the colour of the line you'll get once you click on it. Change the value of the y: position, increasing it by 25 each time, then change the Color and Brightness effects to bring in a new colour. Finally, set the Colour variable in the second stack to match. It's best to leave

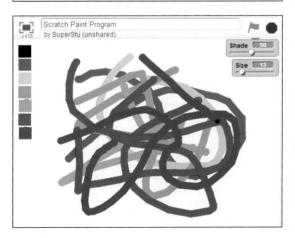

the Shade variable set at 50, and the Brightness effect at 100. To create this little palette, we've set the rest of the colours to 30, 50, 90, 120 and 150. You can always choose different colours, or duplicate and change as many sprites as you have room for.

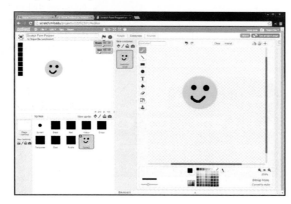

STEP 18
It's not just lines you can paint, however. You can also use the Stamp block to paint with the sprites themselves. First, you need to add a new sprite, either by choosing one from the library or by painting one yourself with the aid of the Costumes Editor. Here's one we made earlier.

STEP 19
Now right-click on the costume in the list just to the left of the Costume Editor and select Duplicate. Drag the duplicate over Sprite 1 where it sits in the Sprites area, then release the mouse button. This copies and transfers this costume

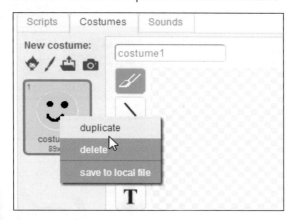

over to Sprite 1 – your main painting sprite. You'll need it later.

STEP 20
Click the Scripts tab. This sprite needs two stacks of script. The first, which starts with 'when green flag clicked', changes the size of the sprite then moves it so that it fits neatly underneath your Colour Palette. You might need to try different values here before you get it right. The second tells the program to broadcast a message when this sprite

is clicked. Here, we're calling it 'smiley'. Again, you're transforming a sprite into a button.

STEP 21
But what happens when that button is clicked? Well, go back to the first sprite you made. We need to make some changes to its script. Click on the 'forever' block underneath the 'when green flag clicked' block and drag the rest of the stack away from the top two blocks. Now you need to add two more blocks to the top stack: a 'switch costume to' block and a 'broadcast message' block. The costume should be set to 'costume1', and you need a new message, which we'll call 'normal brush'.

STEP 22
Now get a 'switch costume to' block and place it on top of the rest of the stack. Change the costume to read 'costume1'. Next, get a 'stop' block from Control, set it to

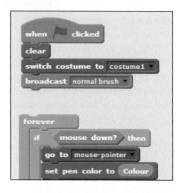

'other scripts in sprite', and place that on top. Finally, get the 'when I receive message' block from the Events category, and click it into place on top. Change the message to 'normal brush'. This script now changes costume to the first costume and draws lines when it gets the normal brush message, just like it did before.

STEP 23 Start a new stack with the 'when I receive message' block, but this time change the message to read 'smiley'. The stack underneath is a variation on the one we've

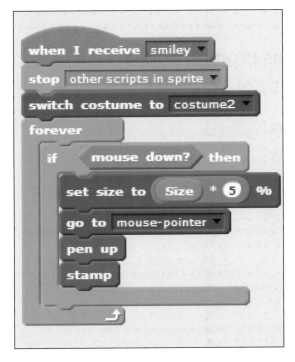

already created to draw lines, but this time it uses the 'stamp' block. This places a copy of the current costume everywhere you click, or draws with the costume if you hold down the mouse button. Note the operator with the Size variable in the 'set size to' block. This allows the Size slider to control the size of the stamp, but adjusts for the fact that the 'set size to' block works differently to the 'set pen size to' block.

STEP 24 Finally, you need to go through each sprite that you use in the palette and add a 'broadcast message' block at the end of the 'when this sprite clicked' stack. Set the message to 'normal brush' and you're all set to draw away. ●

MESS AROUND

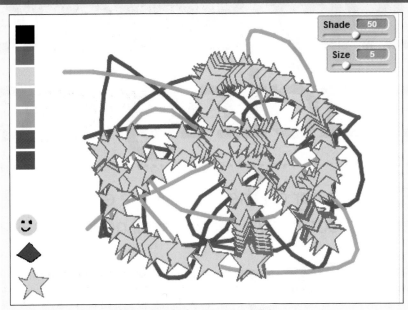

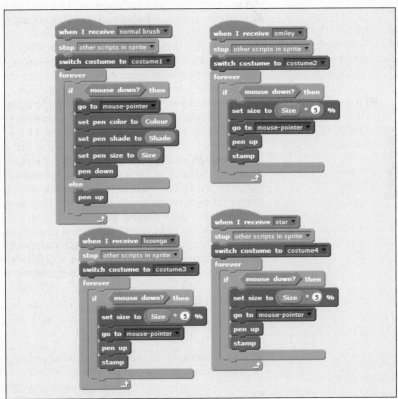

Why stop at one sprite? You can keep adding or painting new sprites and using them to paint with by following steps 18 to 24. You can even drag or duplicate scripts from one sprite to another to save time, adjusting whatever settings and message names need to be altered. Why not try different shapes and patterns, and see what works and what doesn't?

My Scratch racing game

Putting a car on the track is the easy part of this project, but to put it up against some rival racers we'll need to make use of Scratch's lists

> How to use
> Motion blocks
> and variables
> to move a car
> around a track

> How to control
> how a sprite
> behaves with
> colour

> How to time
> things in
> Scratch

> How to make
> and use lists

This top-down racing game seems pretty simple, with just a few sprites racing around a flat 2D track. In fact, there's a little more to it. Most racing games feature some kind of opposition, which usually means coding in artificial intelligence routines to control where they drive, how fast they go, and what they do when they're near to the player's car. This is the sort of problem professional game developers face every day, but with Scratch it's different. Not only are these routines very difficult to code, but the code required might slow Scratch down to a crawl.

That's why this racing game – we'll call it Ghost Racer – cheats. Instead of controlling the rival racers, it memorises how the player races, then puts cars on the track that follow the same patterns. It all works thanks to lists, which store the player's direction and speed in memory, then recall that information to control three 'ghost' cars.

This is going to be a pretty complex project, and before you tackle any complex project you should jot down what you need to do, as this will help you structure the program. In this case, we need to:

❶ Build a racetrack

❷ Put a car on the track

❸ Create controls for how the car will speed up, slow down and steer on the track

❹ Define what will happen when the car comes off the track

❺ Track lap times

❻ Let the player know when they have a new record

❼ Create lists to capture what the car does

❽ Put our ghost racers on the track

❾ Use the information stored in the lists to keep those racers on the track

❿ Define what happens when our car hits a ghost racer

That's quite a lot to be getting on with, so let's get started.

STEP 1 Before we do anything else, we need a track. You can paint this yourself by clicking on the 'Paint new backdrop' button and using the Backdrop Editor. Use the Paintcan tool to fill the whole space with green, then paint on a black road with a nice, thick, black brush. Set the size of the brush to maximum, and paint your track straight on to the green background.

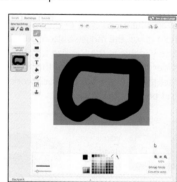

STEP 2 Next, we need a sprite for our car, Why not click on the 'Paint new sprite' button and make your own? Here's one we've made from a series of ellipses, but you can make anything you fancy. Just have fun, and let your imagination run wild.

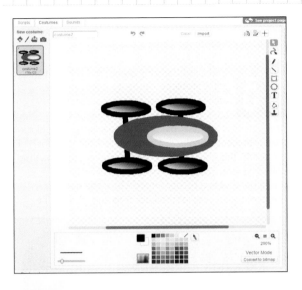

STEP 3

Before we can put our car on the track, we need to create some variables. Go to Data, and create two new ones. Have them marked 'For all sprites', and call them 'lap count' and 'speed'.

STEP 4

Now we start assembling our main control stack for the player's car. This first set of blocks changes the car sprite to a suitable size for our course (10%), puts it in the right place (x: 0, y: 98), pointing it in the right direction (-90), and sets the Speed variable to 0. Our car is in position – it just needs some code to make it go.

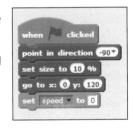

STEP 5

Start by pulling in a Forever loop and adding it to the bottom of the stack. Inside that goes an 'if, then, else' block. Drag a 'key x pressed?' block from Sensing into the space next to the 'if', and set the key to the up arrow. Now grab a 'change variable by x' block from Data, and pull this into the space underneath the 'else'. Set the variable to 'speed' and the value to -0.2. This tells the car to slow down gradually if the up arrow key isn't being pressed.

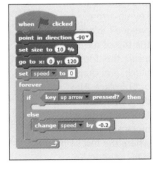

STEP 6

If it's being pressed, we want the car to accelerate, but if it goes too fast, players won't be able to control it. That's why we now drag in another 'if, then, else' block and nest it inside the 'if' section of the last one. For the 'if' condition, we use the 'x > x' operator block and the Speed variable to tell the program that if the Speed variable is higher than 6 it needs to keep speed set to 6. Whatever happens, the speed can't creep up above this level.

STEP 7

Next, add a 'change variable by x' block into the space below the 'else', and set the variable to 'speed' and the value to 0.2. If the current value of speed is below 6 and the up arrow key is being pressed, the value will go up by 0.2. When we've done a little more work, the Speed variable will control the speed of the car, so it will steadily get faster.

STEP 8

What it can't do, however, is steer left or right. Let's fix that. We add two 'if, then' blocks to the bottom of the stack inside the 'forever' loop. The top one uses the 'key x pressed?' block from Sensing to check whether the left arrow key is being pressed, and, if it is, use the 'turn anti-clockwise x degrees' block from Motion to turn 5 degrees anti-clockwise. The bottom 'if, then' block does the same with the right arrow key, but with the 'turn clockwise x degrees' block. Our car can now steer left and right.

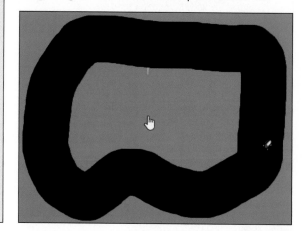

STEP 9

Now we just need to add a few more blocks. The 'if, then' block that goes in next uses the 'x < x' operator to see if the Speed variable is lower than 0.5. If it is, it sets it to 0.5. This stops our car from going backwards if the up arrow key isn't pressed. The next block, the 'move speed steps' block, simply tells the car to move forward in its current direction by the current value of speed. If speed is 6, it will move forwards 6 steps. If it's set to 3, it will move forwards 3

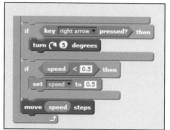

steps. Click the green flag above the Stage, and you can take your car sprite for a spin.

STEP 10

That's got the car moving, but we've still got a problem. At the moment, the car travels just as fast whether it's on the track or not. We can, however, fix this using an 'if, then, else' block and a special Sensing block called 'touching x color?'. Drag the 'touching x color?' block into the space next to the 'if', and click on the little colour square. The normal pointer should change into a hand with a pointy finger. Move the hand over the green grass area of the backdrop and click it. The

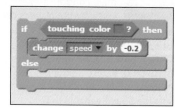

little square should now match the colour. Now drag a 'change variable by x' block into the space underneath, and set the variable to 'speed' and the value to -0.2.

STEP 11

Now it's time for a little bit of rearranging. Click and hold on the 'if key up arrow pressed?' block at the top of the stack inside the 'forever' block, and drag it out of place. Next, drag your new 'if touching x color?' block and place it where the rest of the stack used to be.

ABOUT LISTS

Lists work a bit like variables, but they enable us to store, then use several different bits of data at once. You can use them to hold different pieces of text, like a list of names or a list of replies that a user makes when we ask them to type something in, or we can use them to hold numbers, like a list of answers to sums or a list of coordinates in a game. All we need to do is tell the program where to store the information – as, say, item1 in 'my shopping list' – then we can use the same details to retrieve the information when we need it. In regular programming languages, lists are normally called 'arrays'.

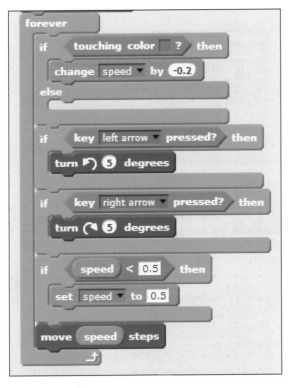

STEP 12 Now grab and drag the 'if key left arrow pressed?' block in the bottom half of your stack away from the blocks above. You need to place this inside the 'forever' block, but outside the 'if, then, else' block.

STEP 13 Finally, grab the rest of the stack and put it in position inside the space beneath the 'else'. You now have a car that accelerates, slows down and steers, and that will drive faster on the track than it will on the surrounding grass. Go on, give it a try!

STEP 14 We have a car that moves, but we don't really have a game. Let's say that the goal in Ghost Racer is to get the lowest lap times. We need a way of tracking when the car completes a lap, and how long it's taken to do it. To do the first bit, we're going to create a new sprite. Just use the 'Paint new sprite' button and the Line tool to draw a yellow line going vertically down the screen. You might want to rename it 'line' and name our car sprite 'car' to make things easier later on.

STEP 15 Once it's finished, grab and drag the sprite into position so that it's just ahead of the car. Now click the Scripts tab. The line sprite's script is pretty simple. We use a 'go to x: y:' block to set its position. The block should have the right values in when you drag it out. The 'if, then' block uses a 'touching x?' operator to see if the line sprite is touching the car sprite, and if it does it will broadcast a new message, which we call 'new lap'. The 'wait 5 secs' block makes sure the new lap message isn't triggered several times as the car crosses the line. Finally, the 'forever' block makes sure that the program is always looking to see whether the car is crossing the line.

STEP 16 In Scratch, you can add scripts to the backdrop, just as you can to any sprite. Click on the Course backdrop next to the Sprites area, and start a new stack with a 'when green flag clicked' block. For now, just add a 'set variable to x' block and set it to 'lap count' and 0. Now start off a second stack with a 'when I receive message' block, setting the message to 'new lap'. Go to Data and grab a 'change variable by x' block and stack this underneath, and set the variable to 'lap count' and the value to 1. This will help us keep track of how many laps our car has finished.

STEP 17 To time our laps, we can use Scratch's own built-in Timer function. Go to the Sensing category and click on the checkbox next to the 'timer' block to make it visible. You might want to move the counter that appears so that it's in the top-left corner of the Stage. Now go to the Data category and create our first list. Click the 'Make a List' button, and call the list 'Lap Times'. Untick the checkbox next to Lap Times to hide the list from view.

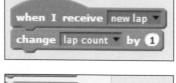

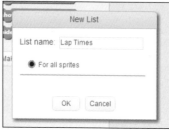

STEP 18 Let's get back to our backdrop script. Add an 'if, then' block to the bottom of the 'when I receive new lap' stack, and drag an 'x > x' operator into place after the 'if'. Drag the block for Lap Times into the first space, and type 1 into the second. This will tell the next few blocks to only start working if the car has completed its first lap. Now grab an 'if, then, else' block and drag this inside.

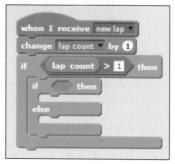

STEP 19 Pull an 'x < x' operator to the space next to the 'if'. Now go to Sensing, and find the 'timer' block. Place this in the first position on the operator. Now go to Data and find the block that says 'item 1 of Lap Times'. Drag this into the second position.

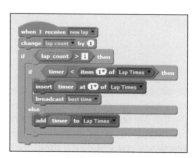

STEP 20 Find the block that says 'insert thing at 1 of Lap Times'. Put this in place in the first gap for the 'if, then, else' block. Drag the 'timer' block into the space where it says 'thing'. Underneath, place a 'broadcast message' block. Select a new message and call it 'best time'.

STEP 21 Now find the block that says 'add thing to Lap Times'. Drag this into position in the second gap of the 'if, then, else' block. Again, drag the 'timer' block into the space where it says 'thing'. What we've just done is tell the program to look at the timer, and see whether the timer for that lap is faster than the best time we've seen so far. If it is, it replaces the best time. If it isn't, it's just added to the list of times. Finally, go to the Sensing category and find the Reset Timer block. Add it to the bottom of this stack. This resets the timer to 0 for the start of every lap.

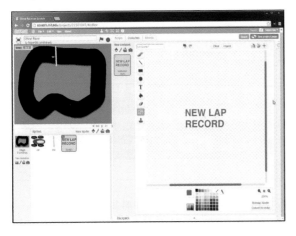

STEP 22 Now create a new sprite by clicking the Paint new sprite button. All we need to do here is use the Text tool and type New Lap Record in a bright colour, as you see here.

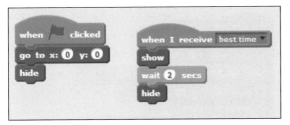

STEP 23 Now click on the Scripts stack and add these two shorts scripts. The first centres the New Lap Record text in the centre of the screen, then hides it. The second waits for the Best Time message, then flashes up the New Lap Record text in the centre of the screen for a couple of seconds, then hides it again.

STEP 24 We have the car moving and we're tracking lap times, but how about some rivals on the track? Well, first we need to create two new lists. For each, go to Data, and

HOW THE GHOSTS WORK

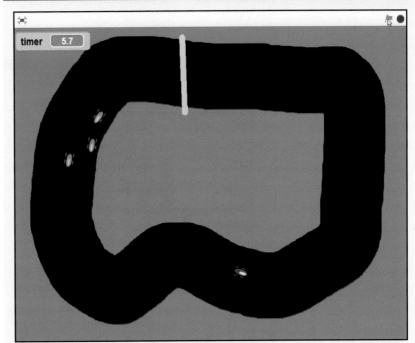

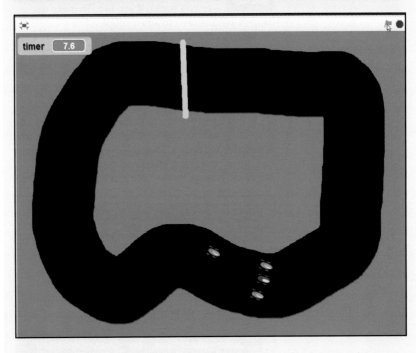

Each time the player car moves, its direction is stored in the Ghost Direction list, while its speed is stored in the Ghost Speed list. When a new ghost is spawned, it looks to item 1 on each list and moves in the direction the Ghost Direction list tells it to at the speed the Ghost List list provides. The Item variable then increases value by 1, so the next time the ghost wants to move it takes its direction speed from item 2 on the list, then item 3, and so on. While its speed isn't quite the same, it's basically copying the player's driving.

click the 'Make a List' button. Call the first list Ghost Direction and the second list Ghost Speed. Untick the checkboxes next to both so the two lists don't clutter up the screen.

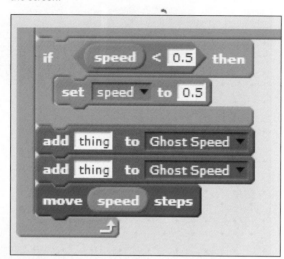

STEP 25
These two lists are going to store data for the player's car's speed and direction, so that the ghost cars can follow in the player's footsteps – or tyre tracks, if you like. To make this happen, we just need to add a couple of new blocks to the player's car's script. Click on the car sprite and scroll down to 'Move speed steps'. Now go to the Data category and drag in two 'add thing to list' blocks, just above it.

STEP 26
First, let's deal with the top one of the two new blocks. Go to the Motion category and look for the 'direction' block at the bottom of the screen. Drag this in where it currently says 'thing' and change the list at the end to 'Ghost Direction'. Now go to the Data category and drag the

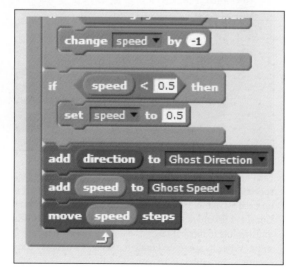

Speed variable to where it currently says 'thing' on the second block. Drop it there, and change the list to read 'Ghost Speed', if it doesn't already.

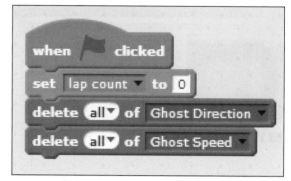

STEP 27
We also need to adjust the script for the backdrop. Look at the 'when green flag clicked' block, and add two 'delete x of list' blocks from the Data category. Set both to delete 'all', and set one to delete all of 'Ghost Speed', and the other to delete all of 'Ghost Direction'.

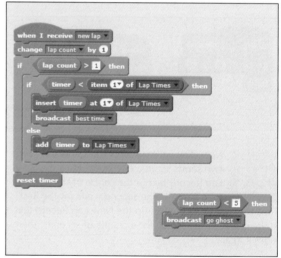

STEP 28
For the 'when I receive new lap' block, we need to create a new 'if, then' block. We set this up so that if the lap count is under 5 then it will broadcast a new message, which we'll call 'go ghost'. Drag this in under the 'if, then, else' block, but still within the 'if lap count > 1' block. We'll use this to spawn new ghost cars once per lap during the second, third and fourth laps.

STEP 29
Now duplicate the main car sprite and call the duplicate 'ghost'. Make double-sure that you have the ghost sprite selected, then delete all the blocks of script in the Scripts area. We need to add three all-new ones. The first tells the ghost car to hide. The second tells the ghost car to

keep listening for the 'go ghost' message. When it receives it, it has to wait 4 seconds, then create a clone of itself.

Place the Item variable in where the item number would usually be, and change the list to 'Ghost Direction'.

STEP 32 The second block is almost a repeat, but using a 'move x steps' block and the Ghost Speed list. However, we want to slow down our ghosts a bit so our player has to make their way through them. That's why we use an 'x – x' operator block, with 'Ghost Speed' in the first space and 0.5 in the second. Finally, we use a 'change x by x' block to 'change Item by 1'.

STEP 30 This last script is a bit trickier. First, we need to create a new variable called 'item', and make sure it's set to 'For this sprite only'. Start a new stack with 'when I start as a clone'. Drag a 'show' block into place, followed by a 'change color effect by 50', and two blocks to get the clone in the right position and heading in the right direction. Now go to Data and add a 'set variable to x' block, changing the variable to 'item' and the value to 1.

STEP 33 We're nearly finished, but we'd like to have some kind of penalty for when the player's car hits a ghost car. All it takes is one final 'if, then' block in the scripts for the main car sprite. This tells the car sprite that if it touches the ghost sprite, it has to change its speed by -1. Drag this into place above the 'if speed <0.5 then' block, and you're all finished and ready to race! ●

STEP 31 Next add a 'forever' loop. Inside it sits three more blocks. The first is 'point in direction' from the Motion category. Look at where the value normally sits, and drag in an 'item 1 of list' block from the Data category.

Put yourself in the program

Get Scratch working with your webcam, and you can put your own face in a program or add simple sound and motion controls

We might mostly use webcams for making video calls, but they can also be put to good use in your latest Scratch program. Webcams can be used to capture sprites and backgrounds, allowing you to put just about anyone or anything into your program, or set a game inside your living room. Meanwhile, take a look inside the Sensing script blocks and you'll find a series of blocks that enable you to sense motion using the camera or noise from a microphone, so that your scratch programs can respond to movement, a shout or a handclap from the user. Sounds good? We'll see how it's done with a trio of bite-sized projects.

Project One: Bat Burster

Our first webcam project is a simple game where we'll despatch a swarm of deadly vampire bats with a pointy finger (although, in practice, the game will work with just about anything you can wave in front of the screen).

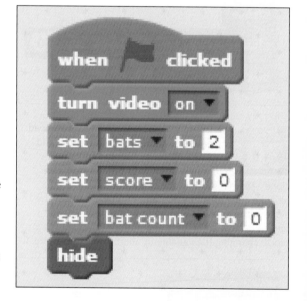

STEP 1 Kick off the project by hitting the 'Choose a new sprite from library' button, and selecting this cartoon bat. Leave the Stage with the default blank backdrop. We'll be filling it in a minute. Now create three variables and call them 'bats', 'score' and 'bat count'. You can set them all to For all sprites.

STEP 2 This initial stack sets the three variables to their starting values and

hides our initial bat. However, it also uses the 'turn video on' block, which you'll find in the Sensing category. This starts the webcam up, and once your webcam kicks in you should see yourself or your surroundings on the screen.

STEP 3 Now click on the Stage, as we want to add a stack here. This one controls the general flow of the game, broadcasting a new message, which we'll call 'go bats' and resetting the timer at the start of each new wave of bats. We allow 10 seconds for the player to get rid of each wave. Once 10 seconds is past, the program will broadcast a 'game over' message. On the other hand, we want to check whether the player has got rid of the last wave of bats. The Bats variable controls how many bats are released in each wave. The bat count tracks how many bats the player has

```
when [flag] clicked
broadcast [go bats ▾]
reset timer
forever
    if < timer > (10) > then
        broadcast [game over ▾]

    if < [bat count] = [bats] > then
        broadcast [go bats ▾]
```

```
when I start as a clone
set size to ( pick random (40) to (80) ) %
show
go to x: ( pick random (-200) to (200) ) y: ( pick random (-160) to (160) )
```

block reveals each clone, then the 'go to' block places each bat in a random location. The x and y settings, -200 to 200 on the horizontal axis and -160 to 160 on the vertical, stop the bats appearing too close to the edges.

squished. When the two numbers are equal, all the bats are gone, so the game calls in a new wave with 'go bats'.

STEP 4
Here's the block that kicks in when that message is triggered. First, it adds 1 to the Bats variable, so that each wave has more bats than the last. Then it resets the Bat count variable to 0 and resets the timer. You've seen the

STEP 6
The second half of this stack uses a Forever loop, then an 'if, then' block, so that the program is constantly checking to see whether the condition we're about to set is being met. In this case, we use the 'x > x' operator block, and drag in the 'video motion on this sprite' block. This

```
when I receive [go bats ▾]
change [bats ▾] by (1)
set [bat count ▾] to (0)
reset timer
repeat [bats]
    create clone of [myself ▾]
```

```
when I start as a clone
set size to ( pick random (40) to (80) ) %
show
go to x: ( pick random (-200) to (200) ) y: ( pick random (-160) to (160) )
forever
    if < ( video [motion ▾] on [this sprite ▾] ) > (20) > then
```

checks whether any motion underneath or around the sprite in question reaches a certain level, which we've set to 20. There's a bit of trial and error here, as so much depends on your webcam and your lighting. Once you have the game up and running, you might want to adjust this variable until the program works properly.

next loop before. It uses the Bats variable to control how many times the loop repeats, and so how many clones of the bat sprite will be created.

STEP 7
When there's enough motion to trigger the 'if, then' block, we get a pop sound, the Bat count variable goes up by 1 and the player's score goes up by 1. Then the clone is deleted.

STEP 5
The next stack starts with the 'when I start as a clone' block, then adds a random element to the size of the bats, so that we'll get some small ones and some big ones. The Show

```
when I start as a clone
set size to ( pick random (40) to (80) ) %
show
go to x: ( pick random (-200) to (200) ) y: ( pick random (-160) to (160) )
forever
    if < ( video [motion ▾] on [this sprite ▾] ) > (20) > then
        play sound [pop ▾]
        change [bat count ▾] by (1)
        change [score ▾] by (1)
        delete this clone
```

Another bat bites the dust! Give the game so far a go, and see how well these primitive motion controls work out.

 STEP 8 Finally, we need to set what happens when the player runs out of time. This last stack brings the original bat sprite to the front, changes the size, then shows a Game Over message for two seconds. It then tells the player what

```
when I receive game over ▼
go to front
go to x: 0 y: 0
set size to 120 %
show
say Game Over for 2 secs
say join You Scored: score for 2 secs
stop all ▼
```

they scored. Here, the Join operator does the work, combining the text in the box after join with the current value of the Score variable as one message. Finally, the 'stop' block, set to 'all', brings our program to a close.

Project Two: **Good Dog!**

Our second project shows off the directional sensitivity of the Video sensing blocks. We've already seen the 'video motion on this sprite' block, but you can also set this to sense video direction. This works the same way as Scratch's sprite direction, so 0 is up, 90 is right, 180 is down and -90 is left. In this case, we're just going to focus on moving left and right, with an animated dog we can push along in either direction with a gesture.

STEP 1 The project begins by importing a sprite from the library. Here, we're going to use Dog2, though any sprite with a walking animation will work. Again, there's no need for any backdrops, as the video feed from the webcam will fill in instead.

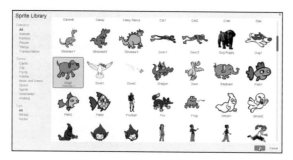

STEP 2 The first stack puts the dog in position and ensures the rotation style is set to 'left-right', so that our dog only moves along a horizontal line. We then grab two video-friendly blocks from the Sensing category. The top one switches on the webcam. The second sets video

```
when 🏴 clicked
go to x: 0 y: 0
set rotation style left-right ▼
turn video on ▼
set video transparency to 0 %
broadcast walkies ▼
```

transparency to 0, so that the dog appears on top of the video feed, with no visible background whatsoever. Finally, the 'broadcast message' block sends a new message, 'walkies', which will start the stack that controls the dog's movement.

STEP 3 Here's the start of the 'walkies' stack. The 'forever' block keeps the blocks inside at work while the program is running, and we use an 'if, then' block just to check whether there's any motion on the webcam. If your webcam is being oversensitive, you can use the value here to make it a bit less sensitive. Just keep pushing the value up so

```
when I receive walkies ▼
forever
    if video motion ▼ on this sprite ▼ > 10 then
        if on edge, bounce
```

that the dog only moves when you want it to. Finally, the 'if on edge, bounce' block makes the dog turn around if or when he hits the edge of the screen.

STEP 4 We can now start constructing the rest of the stack. It's controlled by an If, then loop with an 'x > x' operator. Into this goes a 'video x on x' block from the Sensing category, which checks whether the direction of any movement around the sprite is moving left or right. If it's moving right, this chunk of script makes the dog face right and walk right,

```
if  video direction ▼ on this sprite ▼ > 0  then
    point in direction 90▼
    change x by 20
    play drum 3▼ for 0.25 beats
    switch costume to dog2-a
    change x by 20
    play drum 14▼ for 0.25 beats
    switch costume to dog2-b
```

using the kind of animation we used in our cartoon project earlier on.

STEP 5
Here's the second chunk of the stack. This does exactly the same thing, but it checks for movement going left, then turns the dog around and puts him walking left. Notice the

```
if  video direction ▼ on this sprite ▼ < 0  then
    point in direction -90▼
    play drum 3▼ for 0.25 beats
    change x by -20
    switch costume to dog2-a
    play drum 14▼ for 0.25 beats
    change x by -20
    switch costume to dog2-b
```

drum beats. These help control the speed of the walk and add a little noise to the animation, too.

STEP 6
The two chunks stack together, then the whole caboodle fits inside the first 'if, then' block. Give the program a spin. The dog should move left or right according to the

ABOUT VIDEO TRANSPARENCY

You can use the 'set video transparency to x' block to decide how much or how little of the video feed will be visible in the finished program. Set it to 0 and any sprites will be overlaid directly on the view from your webcam. Set it to 100 and you'll get the backdrop of the Stage with no video showing through. You can still use your webcam for motion control, but you won't see anything it's pointing at.

```
when I receive walkies ▼
forever
    if  video motion ▼ on this sprite ▼ > 10  then
        if  video direction ▼ on this sprite ▼ < 0  then
            point in direction -90▼
            play drum 3▼ for 0.25 beats
            change x by -20
            switch costume to dog2-a
            play drum 14▼ for 0.25 beats
            change x by -20
            switch costume to dog2-b

        if  video direction ▼ on this sprite ▼ > 0  then
            point in direction 90▼
            change x by 20
            play drum 3▼ for 0.25 beats
            switch costume to dog2-a
            change x by 20
            play drum 14▼ for 0.25 beats
            switch costume to dog2-b

    if on edge, bounce
```

movement of your hand. Remember, if it's not working, keep adjusting the value of the 'video motion sensing' block at the top of the stack.

STEP 7
We're not finished yet, though. Did you know that Scratch can listen through your webcam or our laptop's microphone as well as watch? This last stack uses the 'loudness' block from Sensing. If this goes above the threshold we

```
when 🏁 clicked
forever
    if  loudness > 20  then
        stop other scripts in sprite ▼
        switch costume to dog2-c ▼
        think Hmm... for 2 secs
        play sound dog1 ▼ until done
        broadcast walkies ▼
```

▶ Have fun taking your animated dog for walkies with simple hand gestures!

set using the 'x > x' operator, it stops all the other scripts running for a minute, changes the dog's costume to put it in a listening pose, makes him think 'hmm…' and then makes him woof. Broadcasting the walkies message gets him back moving left and right again.

Project Three: **Become a Space Invader**

A webcam is great for simple motion control projects, but it's also brilliant if you want to bring objects, places or people from real life into your programs. Here, we're going to adapt our earlier Starfish Storm project and show you how to transform your mum, dad or mates into menacing space invaders.

STEP 1 First, you need to open up your Starfish Storm project. Go to the My Stuff page and click the See Inside button underneath the project. We don't want to permanently change the original, so click on the File menu and select Save as a Copy.

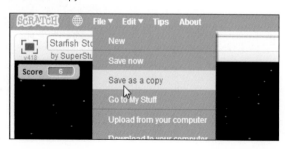

STEP 2 Now click on the main Starfish sprite, then on the Costumes tab. Look above the list of costumes and click on the Camera button to create a 'New costume from camera'. A window will appear showing you the current view from your webcam. Get yourself into position, then click the Save button.

STEP 3 You'll want to edit this costume before you start using it. Choose the Select button from the toolbox on the left, then drag the box over the square or rectangular area of the image you'd like to keep. When you're done, press the Ctrl+C

keys at the same time. This copies the selected chunk of photo into memory.

 STEP 4 Now press the Clear button to empty the editing screen, then press Ctrl+V at the same time. Your selected chunk of photo will pop back into view. Position it over the cross in

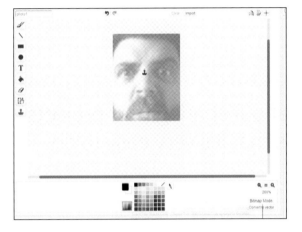

the middle of the Selecting screen, click to place it, then tap the Esc key.

 STEP 5 You can edit the new costume if you want, adding neat little touches like devil horns, glasses, weird eyebrows or a nice moustache. For now, though, we'll leave it as it is. In this case, there's only one costume and there's no need to fiddle around with 'switch costume' blocks. If you need to, though, you can always add them to your script stacks, making sure they point to the costume you've just created (called 'photo1' unless you change it).

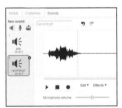 **STEP 6** You don't have to stop at the webcam photos, however. Why not bring in samples of your own voice? Click on the Sounds tab, then the microphone-shaped button,

'Record new sound'. You'll see the Sound Editor. Press the round Record button to record, the square Stop button to stop and the Play button to play things back.

 **STEP 7** You can also click and drag on the soundwave in the window to highlight a section of your sound, then use the Edit menu to trim or copy sections. You can also add simple fade-in, fade-out or volume effects. Here, we're just cutting out unwanted sections from our sample.

 **STEP 8** When you've finished tinkering, you can simply change the 'pop' noise the invaders make when they're blasted to your new sample (recording1 unless you change it). Every time they're shot, you'll hear the noise – better make it a blood-curdling scream, then! ●

ANIMATE YOURSELF

You can always create simple animations by using the webcam to make a number of costumes of the same face in different poses or animations. You can then use an animation script like the one here to switch between the costumes at the right speed.

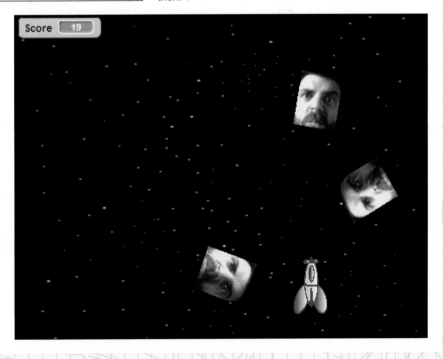

Share your projects

Scratch isn't just about building projects, but about sharing your projects with the Scratch community. The great thing is that it's very easy to do

> How to share projects

> How to use tags to help other users find your work

> What studios are, and why you should use them

When you finish a project and you're proud of it, it's only natural to want to share it, whether that's with your family, your friends or all the other kids at school. Scratch makes that easy, but it also goes much, much further. Community is an important thing in Scratch, and enthusiastic scratchers, as they're called, like to share their work with other scratchers, not just so they can try a program out or play a game, but so that they can look at the code, maybe learn from it, or even suggest improvements. In fact, scratchers will even remix each other's projects, making them work more efficiently, or adding features and ideas that the original author might not have thought about.

Because Scratch itself is web-based, sharing a project is extremely easy. All it takes is a few clicks, and your projects could be being enjoyed and remixed by a legion of keen scratchers.

Sharing a project

STEP 1
You can actually share a project at any time while you're working on it. Look at the top right of the main Scratch project interface and you'll see two buttons: 'Share' and 'See project page'. Click Share and your project will be shared, and accessible by anyone.

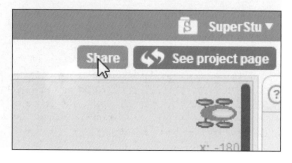

STEP 2
All the same, it's more useful if you set up a proper project page with any notes on the program, and any information on the controls or how to use it. If you're in the project

interface, just click on the 'See project page' button. If you're in the My Stuff page, just click on the project's name, where it's written in blue.

STEP 3
The left-hand side of the project page is dominated by a window, where clicking the green flag button will start your program running. On the right-hand side are two

textboxes, with one for instructions, and one for notes and credits. Click in a box to start typing. Use the Instructions box to tell users what a project does or how to win the game, and also note down any keys that need to be pressed.

 STEP 4 Use the Notes and credits box to mention any ideas about the program, and to credit any games, programs, projects or scratchers that inspired it or have helped while you were

trying to code it. The Scratch community is a caring, sharing kind of place, so if you've found something useful by looking at someone else's program it's only fair to give them credit.

Keys:
Left Cursor: Left
Right Cursor: Right
Up: Accelerate

Braking is for cowardly custards!

Notes and Credits
This is a simple top-down 2D race game in the style of the old arcade classic Super Sprint. I didn't know how to build a proper AI, so I had the idea of tracking the player's car and using the data from there to control some rival racers. It all works pretty well, but the game has a nasty habit of slowing down in full-screen mode on some PCs.

 STEP 5 You can enter Project Tags in the box to help other scratchers find your project. You can only post a maximum of three, so think about them carefully. Basic categories like games or animation are already set up for you to pick, so try to give one to every project. Here, we're going for games, 'racing' and 'cars'. When you're done, press the Share button at the top and your project is shared.

cars x   racing x   games x

 STEP 6 The bar along the bottom has options that scratchers can use when they look inside or try your project. The Star allows them to bookmark your project, so they can find it easily later. The Heart is used to tell you and fellow scratchers that they like your project. You can see who has liked or bookmarked your project from the numbers.

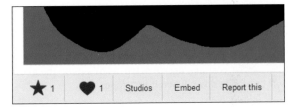

★ 1   ♥ 1   Studios   Embed   Report this

The Studios button allows a scratcher to put your project in a studio (see above), while the Embed button is used to embed the project in another website, like a school website or a blog. Finally, 'Report this' is used to report any content that might break the law or upset someone. Still, you wouldn't do anything like that, would you?

ABOUT STUDIOS

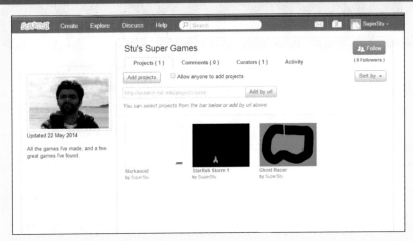

Studios are collections of projects, organised by a type or a theme, or just by the fact that whoever runs the studio likes them. Anyone can create a studio by going to the My Stuff page and clicking the '+ New Studio' button. You can change the picture, add a description, then start adding projects to your studio. These don't have to be your own projects. If you like someone's work, you can add it to your studio and point other scratchers to it. Scratch users can follow other users and keep track of their new projects, but also follow studios, so by setting up a good studio full of good projects you can help promote the best.

Once you've created a studio, you can also invite people to work as curators on it. This empowers them to add projects or remove them from your studio, so you could have a whole team of you working together, adding your own projects to a studio or finding great projects to share. If you have a few friends using Scratch, it's a great idea.

 STEP 7 The two icons at the right of the bar tell you how many scratchers have viewed your project, and keep track of any remixes. Click on this button and you can see any remixes listed, plus any remixes of those remixes. Produce something really good, and you might start a whole family of offshoots.

STEP 8 Once you've shared a project, others can leave comments on it. The Scratch community tends to be friendly, but if you get mean or snarky comments, you can turn off commenting with a quick tick in the checkbox. The two areas on the right list the most recent remixes, or any studios this project has been added to. ●

Remix your projects

If you can see inside a project, you can change and potentially improve it. Welcome to the wonderful world of Scratch remixes!

As we mentioned before, the Scratch community isn't just about sharing completed projects, but about sending projects out into the community so others can help you with a problem, improve your code, or add exciting, new features. It's even possible to take a project you like and use it as the basis for your own project; it's not stealing as long as you make sure the author gets credit. Scratch makes this easy with its concept of remixing.

Remixes are versions of a project, usually made by a different scratcher, that might alter the original project. Scratch automatically tracks remixes as they're created, so that everyone can see which projects started where, and how many remixes a project has inspired.

Remixing the Ghost Racer game

STEP 1 Another scratcher, NinjaBee, has found our Ghost Racer game. She's played around with the game a little, and wants to see how it ticks. Having left a cheeky comment, all she needs to do is click the See inside

button to have a look at all the backdrops, sprites and code.

STEP 2 She can now see the code and even change it, but she can't save any changes to our original version. If she wants to do anything to the game, she needs to press the orange Remix button and start her own remix. If she does so, she'll see this message.

STEP 3 NinjaBee has decided to take the game's title literally, and change the costume for our ghost car sprites to ghosts. She's turned the costume upside down, as otherwise the ghost will be upside down when it first appears.

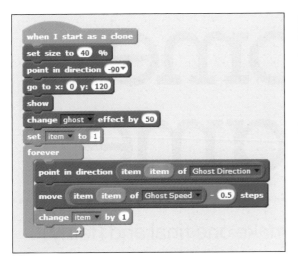

MAKE YOUR OWN REMIX

Why not make your own remix of the Ghost Racer game (or KillerBee's alternative)? Change the top speeds of the car or the speed of the ghost cars. Change the variables to put more ghosts on the track. Try different backdrops with different track layouts, or add two types of ghost car with different speeds. Try adding a brake control or engine noises to the game. The beauty of remixing is it's easy to come up with your own version.

Here, we've made a few changes to the scripts for the Stage and the New Lap Record sprite, as well as giving the New Lap Record a new costume to say Game Over. See if you can see what we've done, and work out what we're trying to do. Is there any way you could do it better? Why not give it a try?

 STEP 4
Now she's messing around with the ghost's script. She's added a 'Set size to x?' block to make the ghosts larger and changed the colour effect to a ghost effect. We've now got big ghosts you can actually see through racing around on the track.

 STEP 5
That's not all. She altered the Go Ghost script, so that the ghosts only wait two seconds before spawning, and changed the operator block and the values in the

'move' block at the bottom of the 'when I start as a clone' script. The ghosts are now travelling faster than the car.

STEP 6
And now she's changed the script for the car sprite so that, when a ghost catches up with it, it plays the 'zoop' sound and loses speed altogether. You're no longer trying to race your way through

the ghost cars, but instead trying to speed away from actual ghosts!

STEP 7
With her remix finished, KillerBee is off to the project page, where she changes the instructions, notes and credits before sharing her remix with a click of the Share button. The finished project page looks something like this. ●

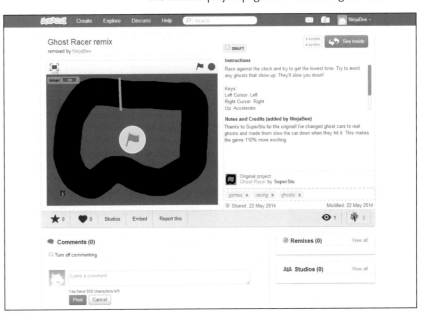

My awesome Scratch game

It's time to harness all of our Scratch skills to make one final and (fairly) awesome retro-style arcade game

Colour Clash is a retro-style arcade game where the player pilots a triangular starship that leaves a destructive, red trail. Your objective is to destroy the fiendish, blue starships by enveloping them in your trail. Your ship runs on energy, which you capture from the blues when you destroy them. Run out of it and it's game over. Destroy enough of the blue ships, however, and you'll launch a new wave, giving you a handy energy boost and even more blue starships to destroy. The only complication? Hitting the blue starships saps your energy. You might survive the odd brush, but do it too often and you'll find yourself out of gas.

OK, so it's not exactly Minecraft, let alone Super Mario, but what do we need to make it work?

1 A red starship that leaves a deadly trail

2 Blue starships to destroy

3 An energy meter

4 A way of launching new waves and setting how many blue starships will be in each wave

5 A way of keeping score

6 When a blue starship hits the energy trail, they need to be destroyed, boosting the score and the player's energy

7 When the red starship hits a blue starship, it needs to lose energy

8 When all the blue starships are destroyed, we need a new wave

9 When the red starship runs out of energy, we need to end the game and say 'game over'.

That's a pretty good working framework, so let's put it into action.

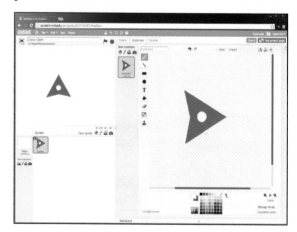

STEP 1
We'll start by setting up the sprite the player will control. Press the 'Paint new sprite' button and create it line by line. Our design is deliberately simple, but if you want something different, go ahead.

STEP 2
We'll start by getting the movement right. We're going to handle our ship using the mouse, and control its speed with a variable, so we need to go to Data and hit the Make a Variable button, and call that variable 'speed'. Once

that's done, we start off with the necessary blocks to set the size, the starting position and the starting direction.

```
when space key pressed
set size to 25 %
go to x: 0 y: 0
point in direction 0
```

STEP 3

This is the basic movement stack for the ship. It's actually a variation of the script we used in the racing game, but instead of using the cursor keys to control direction, the ship points in the

```
when space key pressed
set size to 25 %
go to x: 0 y: 0
point in direction 0
forever
    if  speed > 4  then
        set speed to 4
    else
        if  mouse down?  then
            change speed by 0.5
        else
            change speed by -0.05

    if  speed < 0  then
        set speed to 0

    point towards mouse-pointer
    move speed steps
```

direction of the pointer and accelerates when we press the mouse button. If you take a good look at the stack, you can see how we use the Speed variable to control the speed of movement, and how pressing the mouse button (the 'if mouse down' condition) increases the speed to a maximum of 4.

STEP 4

Now we need to put the trail in place. For this, we use Scratch's Pen feature, just like we did in the Pattern Generator project earlier. You can see where we've put the three green pen blocks so that, when the mouse if pressed, a line is

```
when space key pressed
set size to 25 %
go to x: 0 y: 0
point in direction 0
clear
forever
    if  speed > 4  then
        set speed to 4
    else
        if  mouse down?  then
            change speed by 0.5
            set pen color to 60
            set pen size to 2
            pen down
        else
            change speed by -0.05
            pen up
```

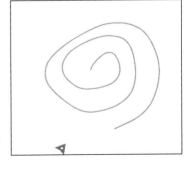

drawn with the pen colour set to 60 and the size to 2. We've also put a 'pen up' block below the 'else', so that the pen won't draw if the ship isn't accelerating, and a 'clear' block near the top of the stack, to clear the Stage of lines every time we run the program. Give the program so far a try. Press the green flag, then press the space key.

STEP 5

With the ship up, speeding around the Stage and leaving a trail, it's time to start work on the rest of the game. First, click on the 'paint new backdrop' icon and fill the Stage with black paint using the Paintcan tool. We're going to need this later. Now click on the Scripts tab, as we're going to control some of the core game functions from the Stage itself. Now we need to set up four new variables, which all of our sprites will share. We'll call them 'EnemyCount', 'Energy', 'WaveCount' and 'Score'. Set them all to 'For all sprites' as you make them.

STEP 6
Here's the Stage's main stack. As you can see, the first chunk just sets up the different variables, then broadcasts a new message, which we'll call 'new wave'. The second chunk is a 'forever' loop that checks for two conditions.

```
when space key pressed
set Score to 0
set WaveCount to 2
set EnemyCount to 0
set Energy to 1000
broadcast new wave
forever
    if  WaveCount = EnemyCount  then
        set EnemyCount to 0
        broadcast new wave

    if  Energy < 0  then
        broadcast game over
```

In this game, we track the number of enemies launched in each wave with the variable WaveCount and the number of enemies destroyed by the player with the variable EnemyCount. The first 'if, then' block checks whether all the enemies in the wave have been destroyed, then launches a new wave. The second tracks the player's Energy, and if it slips below 0 broadcasts a 'game over' message, which will launch a whole Game Over routine.

IMPROVING PERFORMANCE

Certain things really slow Scratch down. Have too many 'forever' loops in a program and you can slow it to a crawl. Keep applying different colour or ghost effects to too many sprites or clones, and your whole program can slow down. If a program you're writing is running badly, have a good look through and see if you can find ways of making it more efficient. For example, you might find you have two sprites set to detect each other when you only need one, or you might have instructions running when a sprite is still that only need to be running when it's moving. By fixing these issues, you could speed up your program. We call this process optimisation.

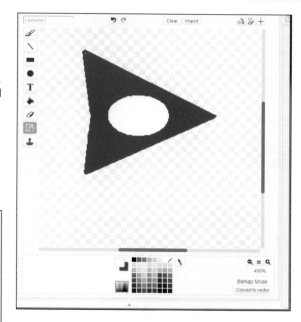

STEP 7
OK. Let's put some enemies on the screen. Again, the sprite is a pretty simple design, and the first stack isn't too complex, either. It tells the sprite to scale to 30%, then hide, waiting to spawn a small army of clones.

STEP 8
This is where our second stack kicks in. This waits for the 'new wave' message. This first clears any pen lines from the Stage, then changes WaveCount so that this new wave will spawn one more enemy ship than the last wave. The 'change Energy' block gives the player's Energy level a boost, and after that the 'repeat' block creates clones according to the current value of WaveCount. If WaveCount = 3, then three clones will be spawned. If WaveCount = 4, four clones will be spawned, and so on.

```
when I receive new wave
clear
change WaveCount by 1
change Energy by 200
repeat WaveCount
    create clone of myself
```

STEP 9
But what happens when they're spawned? First of all, we want them to spawn in a random location, facing a random direction. As always, we do this by putting 'pick

```
when I start as a clone
go to x: pick random -220 to 220  y: pick random -160 to 160
point in direction pick random -180 to 180
show
```

random' blocks in the x, y and 'direction' spots on the 'go to' and 'point in direction' blocks. The 'show' block then reveals the brand-new clone.

STEP 10
Next, we're going to use a 'repeat until' block. This block keeps on doing the same things until a certain condition is met. Here, it's when the sprite touches something green, like the line being drawn by the player's spaceship. To set the block to this colour, run the

program and trace some green lines around the Stage. Stop the program, then click on the little square in the 'touching color x?' block. Now, being very careful, click on a green line to sample the colour. If you look, you'll see that the colour of the little square changes colour as it's over certain colours. Just watch for it to turn green as you move the mouse around, then click.

STEP 11
When the ship hits the trail, we want it to disappear, adding 1 to the EnemyCount and Score variables, and giving the player's ship a small energy boost. All it takes are three 'change variable by x' blocks and a 'delete this clone' block, which we put last to make sure the other blocks have time to run. We also add a 'play

MAKING BLOCKS

Making your own blocks to define subroutines can be incredibly useful. You save yourself work as you don't need to keep adding the same blocks over and over again, but you can also make your program more efficiently. Think carefully about your program, and ask yourself whether there are instructions that it might be doing over and over again, and whether you can cut these down by producing custom blocks, and using those instead.

sound' block and set it to the 'pop' effect, which is added automatically to every new sprite. This whole stack attaches to the bottom of the 'repeat until' loop, as we don't want any of these things to happen until our cloned enemy ship hits a green line.

STEP 12
Until that happens, we just want the enemy ships to move. That's handled by a Turn block and a Move block from the Motion category, along with an If on edge, bounce block. We

can change the behaviour of the ships by using different values here. For now, 3 for the 'turn' block and 5 for the 'move' block gives us nice, graceful turns.

STEP 13
We've actually got the basics of the game in place now, but if you try it you'll soon notice one thing: it's all too easy. What we need is risk – the risk that the player's ship will run

out energy, and that this will mean game over. That's easily done. First, add a new 'change variable by x' block to the player ship's main stack, right underneath the 'pen down' block. Set it to 'Energy' and set the value to -5. Now, whenever the ship is accelerating, it's losing energy.

STEP 14
We also want energy to drain away when it hits one of the blue ships. Add another 'if, then' block to the stack, and set it to change 'Energy by -50' when this sprite is touching the enemy sprite.

STEP 15
Now let's make those enemies a little less predictable. First, click on the enemy sprite in the Sprites area, then go to Data and add a new variable. We'll call this 'EnemySpeed', and we need to set it to 'For this sprite only'. Next, slide a new 'set variable to x' block into place near the start of the 'when I start as a clone' stack, just beneath the 'go to' and 'point in direction' blocks. Set it to use the new EnemySpeed variable, and use a 'pick random' block for the value, set to minimum and maximum values of 3 and 6.

STEP 16
Just grab the marker block for the EnemySpeed variable and use it to replace the value in the 'move x steps' block. Each cloned enemy ship will now have its own random EnemySpeed value, which controls how fast that ship will move.

STEP 17
Let's add one final visual flourish. Go to the Pen category and add a 'set pen colour to' block and a 'set pen size to' block to the 'when I receive new wave' stack. Use a 'pick random' block for the value of the first block, set to a minimum of 120 and a maximum of 160. Use a value of 1 for the 'set pen size'.

STEP 18
Next, add a 'change pen color' block and a 'pen down' block to the 'When I start as a clone' stack. Drop them carefully inside the 'repeat until' loop. Now, each wave of enemy

ships will leave a trail with a different colour, and that colour changes as the ship flies around. The colour is set for the whole wave in the 'when I receive new wave' block, then changed by the 'change pen color' block by the stack that moves each clone.

STEP 19
We now have a reasonably tricky game. The next step is to set what happens when the player's Energy hits 0, and the game is over. First of all, we want the sprites to stop what they're

doing, so that the game grinds to a halt. All you need to do is add this stack to each of the sprites, including the Stage, where the 'stop' block should read 'stop other scripts in sprite'.

STEP 20 It's time to create a new sprite using the 'Paint new sprite' button. For this one, you just use the Text tool and type 'Game', then hit the Return key, and type 'Over'. You can

choose whatever colour you like. When you're done, click on the Scripts tab, and we'll start putting together the main Game Over script for our game.

STEP 21 The first stack puts the Game Over message in position at the centre of the screen and reduces the size to 10%. It also adds a Ghost effect, set to 100 to make the message entirely transparent. The Stage is set for a slick effect. The second stack makes the message bigger and less transparent with every repeat, until it pops out, large as life, in the middle of the screen.

STEP 22 That's good, but wouldn't it be better to tell the player what they scored? In fact, wouldn't it be better still if we had some kind of high score table? To pull that off, we're

ADD A NEW WAVE MESSAGE

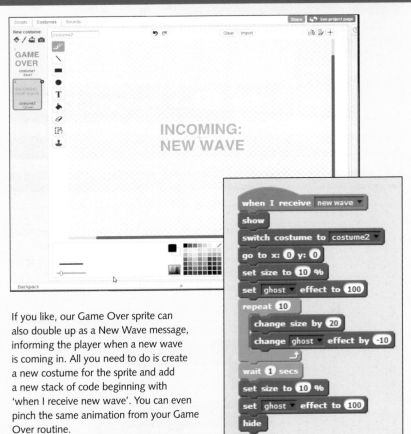

If you like, our Game Over sprite can also double up as a New Wave message, informing the player when a new wave is coming in. All you need to do is create a new costume for the sprite and add a new stack of code beginning with 'when I receive new wave'. You can even pinch the same animation from your Game Over routine.

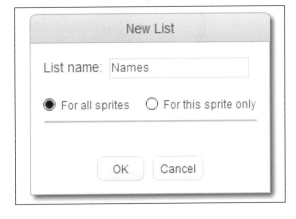

going to have to use lists. Start by making two new lists, which we'll call HighScore and Names. Untick the checkbox next to each list's block to hide it from view.

STEP 23 Pull in an 'if, then, else' block, then add the 'x > x' operator next to the 'if'. Stick the block for the Score variable into the space for the first value, then grab the 'item x of list'

```
change size by 20
change ghost effect by -10
wait 2 secs
if     Score > item 1 of HighScore     then

else
```

```
when I receive game over
show
repeat 10
    change size by 20
    change ghost effect by -10
wait 1 secs
if     Score > item 1 of HighScore     then
    say New High Score! for 1 secs
    ask What's your name? and wait
    insert Score at 1 of HighScore
    insert answer at 1 of Names
else
```

block and put that in where the second should go. Keep the item at 1 and make sure the list is set to 'HighScore'. All we're doing is telling the program to look at the current score and at the current high score, and if the score is higher, to do what we tell it to next.

```
when I receive game over
show
repeat 10
    change size by 20
    change ghost effect by -10
wait 1 secs
if     Score > item 1 of HighScore     then
    say New High Score! for 1 secs
    ask What's your name? and wait
else
```

STEP 24 What's that? Well, first of all we want it to say 'New High Score!', then we want it to ask the player for their name. For that, we use a regular 'say for x secs' block, followed by an 'ask and wait' block from the Sensing category.

STEP 25 The next two blocks then insert the new high score at the top of the HighScore list, and the name that's typed in at the top of the Names list. As long as nothing goes wrong, the two will be linked, so whoever has the highest score – and so the score at position 1 of HighScore – will have their name at position 1 of Names.

STEP 26 It's time to show you one last Scratch trick. We want the game to end with a little high-scores table whether the player has a new high score or not, but why bother adding the same blocks twice? Scratch has a useful Make a Block feature, where we can create a useful stack of code from other blocks, then call that stack – or subroutine in programming language – with a single block. Go to More Blocks, click the Make a Block button

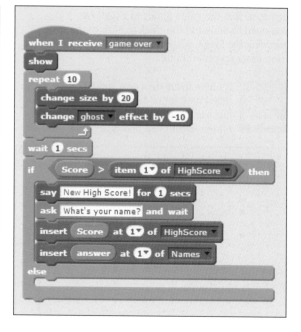

and type 'SayScores' into the box. You'll see that a new block, 'define SayScores', has appeared in the Scripts area.

STEP 27 This first block simply tells the player their score. As you can see, we've used the 'join' operator here. This useful block can be used to join some text and a

```
define SayScores
say join Score: score for 1 secs
say HIGH SCORES for 1 secs
```

variable, or even two variables, in a sentence or a statement. In this case, it says 'Score: ' followed by the current value of the Score variable.

STEP 28
You might remember this next trick from the Racing Game project. Create a variable called 'Item', then add these blocks of script to the bottom of the stack.

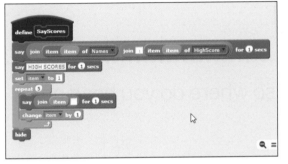

The trickiest bit is the 'say' block, which uses multiple 'join' operators to say the current value of the Item variable, followed by the name of the player it refers to, followed by that player's score. You might need a couple of tries to get this right, so make sure it matches what you see here.

STEP 29
We've defined what the SayScores subroutine is and what it does. Now we can put it to good use. Just drag our new SayScores block into position both at the bottom of the 'if, then' section of the 'if, then, else' block, and the 'else' section. We now get a readout of high scores at the end of every game. Why not give the game a go now? It should be ready for you to play! ●

EXPERIMENT

There are loads of different things you can try out to make this game even better and more exciting. Why not add some sounds? Or how about adding some music? You could also try out different values for the movements of your ship and the enemy ships, or try different amounts of Energy added or lost when you finish a wave or when you collide.

Every change you make will have an impact on the game. If you want to preserve the original, make sure you use Scratch's Save a Copy feature to save one version as your best version, and another version as a testbed for your tinkering. Go on, have some fun and see what you can come up with!

▼ Colour Clash is now ready for action. Give it a go!

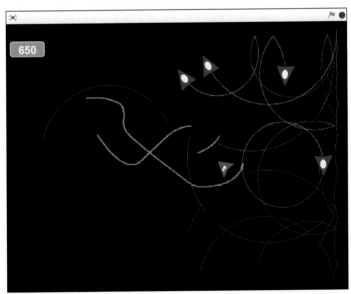

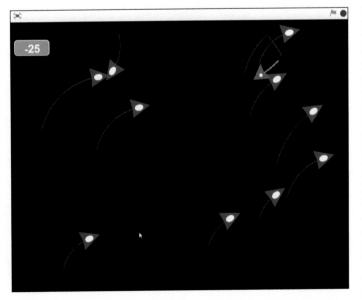

Your next steps in coding

You're well on your way to mastering Scratch, so where do you head next on your programming adventure?

I t might be simple, but Scratch can create a wide variety of games and animations. Eventually, though, you'll want to create something that can work on a bigger screen or at a higher resolution, or can use more advanced graphics or even 3D. That's not a problem if you're ready to move onto a proper textual programming language, but if you're not there are alternatives.

Alice

Like Scratch, Alice is a graphical coding environment designed to introduce novices to the joys of coding. Its tiles work a little like Scratch's blocks, and it's not difficult to move between the two. However, while Scratch is designed to handle 2D games and animations, Alice works with 3D models in 3D scenes. That doesn't mean you can create the next Pixar movie with Alice, but it does mean you'll get a good introduction to 3D graphics as well as simple logic. In fact, the instructions

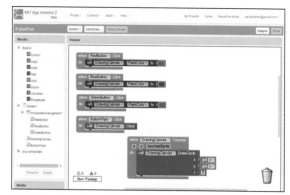

▲ MIT App Inventor is similar to Scratch, but with the bonus that you can produce apps that run on Android smartphones.

used in Alice are designed to reflect the standard statements used in mainstream programming languages like C++, C# and Java. It's a good choice if you want to work with something that's a bit like Scratch, but gives you more to get your teeth into.
● www.alice.org

MIT App Inventor

Developed with the aid of Google, MIT App Inventor might be seen as a 'grown up' Scratch. It's another block-based programming tool, and if you're used to Scratch you'll find a lot that's familiar. It's a lot more complex, not to mention intimidating to start with, but the effort could be worth it. That's because App Inventor produces apps that can run on Android smartphones, so you can use it to produce functional programs. It also means you can play with the built-in features of a smartphone, including the motion sensors, cameras and the touchscreen. If you're starting to outgrow Scratch, App Inventor could be for you.
● appinventor.mit.edu/explore/

▼ Like Scratch, Alice is aimed at programming novices, but instead of 2D it works with 3D models in a 3D environment.

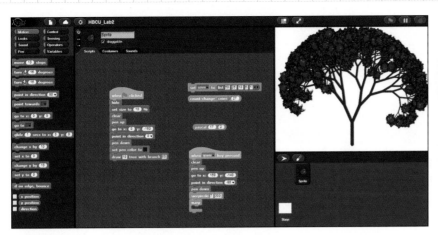

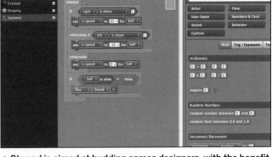

▲ Stencyl is aimed at budding games designers, with the benefit that Stencyl games can run on iOS and Android smartphones.

SNAP!

Formerly known as BYOB (or Bring Your Own Blocks), SNAP! is based on Scratch and could be described as an extended version. It runs along similar lines and uses many of the same blocks, but adds extra capabilities for more advanced coding. Like Scratch, it can run in an ordinary browser window, and runs in JavaScript. SNAP! supports more technical features like first-class functions, functional programming and recursion, which won't mean much to novice coders, but will eventually mean a lot to budding computer scientists. Its user interface and general style make it feel like a Scratch for older students. SNAP! programs can be made faster and more efficient than their Scratch equivalents; you can probably replicate most of what you can do in SNAP! in Scratch, but it might take a little longer and require some ingenuity. It's a great step up from Scratch.
● snap.berkeley.edu/

▲ SNAP! is a great step up from Scratch with extra capabilities for more advanced coding.

Stencyl

Stencyl builds on the principles of Scratch, but adds a mass of features aimed at budding games designers, including editors for sprites, and the tiles and terrain that make up the scenery, plus script blocks that support more of the specific needs of games. Like SNAP!, Stencyl allows you to make your own blocks and share them. It's a little more complex to learn than Scratch, but there are enough similarities to soften the learning curve. Best of all, Stencyl games can run on iOS and Android tablets and smartphones, although the free version will only let you test them. Stencyl has been used to develop successful Flash games, not to mention games on the iTunes App Store and the Google Play Store. If you want to get further as a games developer, Stencyl may be your ticket to the big time.
● www.stencyl.com/

GameSalad Creator

GameSalad Creator is another visual coding tool for games development, where you set up scenes, bring in sprites (or actors), and set up the game logic in a special backstage panel. With its more object-oriented approach and its rules, physics-based properties and behaviours, it works in a different way to Scratch, but it's possible to produce some impressive 2D games, as you can see from the efforts showcased in GameSalad's Featured Games Gallery. What's more, GameSalad games will run on Android, iOS and Kindle devices, although you can't publish Android or Windows games to an app store without an expensive Pro licence. ●
● gamesalad.com/creator

TEXTUAL CODING

These graphical coding environments are great for learning, and great for putting programs together fairly quickly. In the end, though, most novice programmers will have to get their hands dirty with some good, honest code. There are various ways of making the leap, but a handful of environments have been created specifically to help new programmers – and particularly young new programmers – get stuck in. We'll be looking at one of these, SmallBASIC, in the next chapter, but it's also worth looking at Hackety Hack, which uses a graphics toolkit, shoes and a series of lessons to teach you the rudiments of a useful language, Ruby. KidsRuby is another alternative, providing an extremely simple environment for learning the language.

▲ Some impressive 2D games have been produced using GameSalad Creator, as showcased here.

Chapter
3

Section 3
BASIC basics

Learning Scratch is just the start of your journey into code. For our next steps, we're going to have to dive into BASIC. This is a textual programming language with a long and proud history, and one that many novice programmers have cut their coding teeth on. It's easy to learn and follow, but has enough power to build professional apps. While learning BASIC, you'll see how many of the basic coding elements in Scratch are mirrored in a textual language, and you'll also get to grips with syntax, structure and other programming fundamentals. You might not master it all straight away, but you'll be surprised at how easy it becomes with a little practice. Plus, while you're learning the basics, you'll be working on some fun projects that give you scope to try your own ideas.

IN THIS SECTION

Introducing SmallBASIC

If you're ready to move onto a textual programming language, Microsoft's SmallBASIC has you covered with its simplicity and power

Microsoft SmallBASIC is a simple programming language based on BASIC, which stands for Beginner's All-Purpose Symbolic Instruction Code. BASIC languages have been around for years and come in a range of different varieties, and that largely comes down to how simple yet powerful a language it is. SmallBASIC differs from other forms because it contains just 14 keywords. This makes it easier to learn than other versions, yet you can still make exciting applications and amazing games just by learning a little bit of code.

This killer combination of simplicity and power makes SmallBASIC a good first choice for anyone who's interested in becoming a software developer and wants to go further than a visual programming environment like Scratch. It's ideal for learning the basics of programming, and it's been adopted by many primary and secondary school pupils. It also helps that you can think of SmallBASIC as a cutdown version of Microsoft's Visual Basic, the most popular version of the language, and one still used by many professional programmers today. SmallBASIC and Visual Basic share a similar structure and keywords, so if you master SmallBASIC it's easy to transfer your skills and knowledge to Visual Basic.

Where can you find SmallBASIC?

The easiest answer is to go online and head to smallbasic.com. You need to be careful when searching on the internet, as there's another programming language with exactly the same name. Once you get to the website, you'll find that SmallBASIC has an active online community where you can find help and resources, not to mention applications and games to download. The website also hosts some simple tutorials, as well as more detailed documents explaining every aspect of SmallBASIC coding.

Unlike Scratch, which you access over the internet, SmallBASIC needs to be downloaded and installed. You'll find a button for downloading the package at the top right of the website. After you've installed the program, take some time to have a look around the website, as there are many links to support you in getting started or pages

◀ You can download SmallBASIC from the website, then access a huge range of tutorials and sample programs.

> # " Make exciting apps and amazing games just by learning a little bit of code "

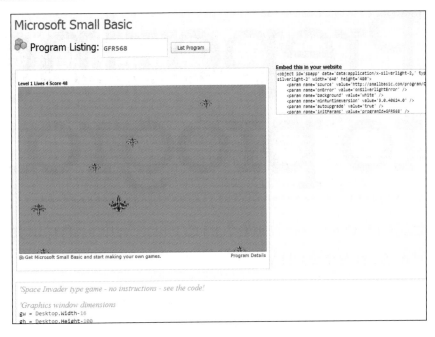

that tell you how to get things done. The PDF tutorial, step-by-step learning curriculum and reference wiki can all be very useful when you're trying to learn, although we're going to give you plenty of help in these pages as well.

How can you use it?

Unlike Scratch, where you drag blocks of code from the Blocks Palette to build your program, the instructions in SmallBASIC – as in most high-end languages – need to be typed manually. This not only means that you'll have to know the keywords, but also that any spelling mistakes or missed symbols will result in your program not compiling and therefore problems with the end result. If there are any errors, the SmallBASIC Editor will tell you what line and position the errors are on, but it's

▲ Hundreds of budding programmers are already using SmallBASIC to create and share their own games and apps.

down to you to solve them. You'll also get a short technical explanation of the problem, but the wording can be hard to decipher if you're new to programming.

Importance of debugging

Fixing these errors, or 'debugging' as programmers like to call it, is a crucial part of coding. You might even find it weirdly satisfying one day. Plus, while this all sounds like a headache, the process really puts you in control. Change your code just a little, and you can make sure the program works the way you want it to, or even make it run more efficiently.

SmallBASIC is classed as a complier language because, when you run the program, the computer will check your code and create a standalone file – a EXE file in Windows – which you can run independently of SmallBASIC on a Windows computer.

Another great feature of SmallBASIC is that, when somebody creates a program or a game, this can be quickly and easily shared with other people online. All you need is an import ID for the program, and you can quickly type in this code. SmallBASIC will download their program for you to test and play, without you having to manually download files and load them yourself.

SmallBASIC on Facebook

You can also have a look at the SmallBASIC group if you have access to Facebook. It's a great place to look at what other users around the world have been making. This would also be a great place to talk about and get feedback on all of the programs that you make (www.facebook.com/groups/smallbasic/). ●

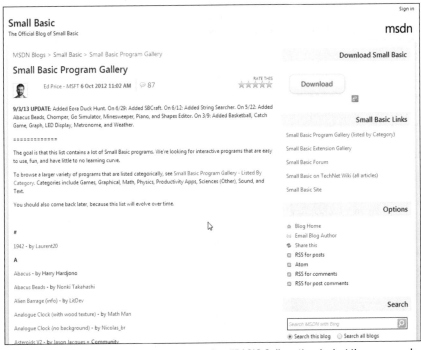

▲ You can find and download programs from the SmallBASIC Gallery, then look at the source code to see what makes them tick.

Preparing to program

Before you can have fun coding with SmallBASIC, you first need to install the software on your PC, and find your way around its simple interface

You can download SmallBASIC by clicking on the Download button in the top-right corner of the website's homescreen.

To install it, you'll need a laptop or PC running Windows XP, Vista, 7 or 8, and you'll also need the Microsoft .NET Framework 3.5 installed. If you haven't got this installed already, you can download it for free from www.microsoft.com/en-us/download/details.aspx?id=21.

Once you've downloaded the installer file, you need to run it to install the program on your PC or laptop's local hard drive. The installer file is a small 5.74MB, and even when the core software is installed it will take only 7.40MB. The programs are even tinier, so you don't have to worry about SmallBASIC taking up too much space on your computer.

Install SmallBASIC in three easy steps

STEP 1 Double-click the installer file and the setup wizard will start automatically. Click Next to continue. The end user licence agreement is a standard legal disclaimer for the use of the

software. Tick 'I accept the terms in the license agreement', then click Next to continue.

STEP 2 The installer selects all the core files and English language resources needed, but in the unlikely event that you need to install additional language translations, just select them from the tree menu. Click Next to continue.

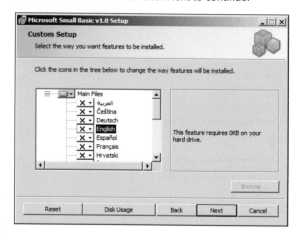

STEP 3 Confirm your installation options by clicking Install, and the program will start the installation. The progress bar will take just a few seconds before it fills, and when it's done

CODING KEYWORDS

IDE: Integrated Development Environment. A software package and user interface that enable and support coding or programming. One IDE might support several different languages.

THE SMALLBASIC TOOLBAR

The SmallBASIC toolbar at the top of the screen gives you instant, easy access to a range of helpful and important features:

1 **New:** Creates a new SmallBASIC program

2 **Open:** Opens an existing SmallBASIC program

3 **Save:** Saves the current program to its current location

4 **Save as:** Saves the current program to a specific location

5 **Import:** Imports a SmallBASIC program using the Program ID from the online community

6 **Publish:** Publishes your program to the internet for others to download

7 **Cut:** Cuts any highlighted text and saves it to the clipboard, ready to use later

8 **Copy:** Copies any highlighted text to the clipboard, ready to use later

9 **Paste:** Pastes any text you saved to the clipboard earlier into the Editor

10 **Undo:** Takes back your last action

11 **Redo:** Brings back whatever it was you last undid

12 **Run:** Executes your code so you can see and test your program

13 **Graduate:** Converts your SmallBASIC program to a full Visual Basic program, so that you can easily carry on working on it when you're ready to get more advanced

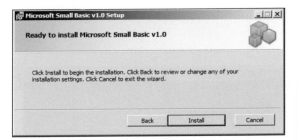

you can complete the installation by clicking the Finish button. Now that you've installed SmallBASIC, you can launch the program by clicking on the Start button, then All Programs, then SmallBASIC in Windows Vista to Windows 7, or by using the Search charm or clicking on the icon in the Apps screen on Windows 8.

Using SmallBASIC

When you first load SmallBASIC, you'll be greeted with a simple interface that's split into three sections. You have a toolbar **1** across the top of the page with the kind of basic features you'll find in any software package, including buttons for Open, Save, Copy and Paste – not to mention the all-important Run to run your program.

The Editor window **2** is the main white area where you'll type your code. This is automatically numbered when you go onto a new line, so if you have an error the debug program will tell you the line followed by the number of characters across.

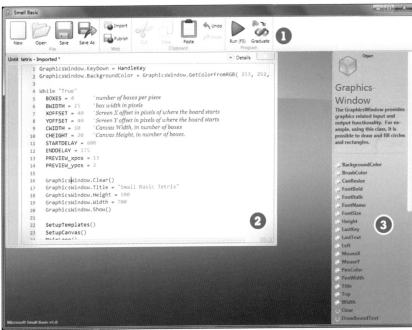

▲ It shouldn't take you long to get used to SmallBASIC's simple interface.

The side panel **3** is a help feature that will give you information about the built-in features in SmallBASIC and their properties. This will change depending on what you click or type in the Editor window, so that you get the most helpful information, where available. ●

My first Small-BASIC program

It's time for our first steps into textual programming with what's probably the simplest program you can possibly write

Let's start by taking SmallBASIC for a test drive. Our first program is a classic exercise in the software development world. Just about everyone does the 'Hello World' program, regardless of what language they're learning. It's the simplest program you can write, as it just displays 'Hello World' back to you in a text window. Still, it's a good way to familiarise yourself with a new environment, and it ensure you can enter text, compile the program and see the results.

Type the following line of code in the editor window:

```
TextWindow.WriteLine("Hello
World")
```

▲ 'Hello World' is the simplest program you can write, and a great way to get used to a new coding environment.

To execute your program, you can click the Run button on the toolbar or press F5 on the keyboard.

Congratulations! You've just written your first program, and you should see the text window with your 'Hello world' statement. SmallBASIC will automatically add a 'press any key to continue' message, which will close the text window and end your first program.

Changing properties

```
TextWindow.Foregroundcolor = "Green"
```

When we call an object in SmallBASIC, we can change the properties of it – the bits that alter its appearance or behaviour. In our example,

TextWindow is the object and Foregroundcolor is one of the properties. Assigned colours need to be in quotation marks: e.g. "Magenta". As an experiment, try replacing "Green" with another colour.

SmallBASIC, like many other programming languages, goes through and processes your code

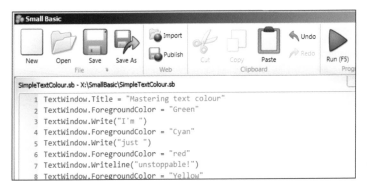

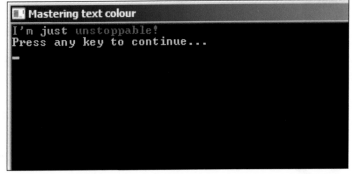

one line at a time in the order that you typed it, so when we assign a colour to the text window it will stick with that colour until the end of the program or until you change it again within the code.

Now let's try to add different colours to our text by entering the code below:

```
TextWindow.Title = "Mastering text colour"
```

```
TextWindow.ForegroundColor = "Green"
```

```
TextWindow.Write("I'm ")
```

```
TextWindow.ForegroundColor = "Cyan"
```

```
TextWindow.Write("just ")
```

```
TextWindow.ForegroundColor = "red"
```

```
TextWindow.Writeline("unstoppable!")
```

```
TextWindow.ForegroundColor = "Yellow"
```

Again, execute your program with the Run button or F5. As you can see, the order in which you type your code is crucial to getting the desired colour effect. The colour change at the end to yellow is for the 'press any key to continue' text. Without that change, it would still be red from the previous word. In this example, we've used the code TextWindow.Write and TextWindow.Writeline.

CODING KEYWORDS

Compile: The process where all the raw code for a program and everything it needs to run is put together as a single file that anyone with the right operating system should be able to run. In Windows, this would be a EXE file.

Execute: To launch your program. This is why many Windows' programs have a EXE suffix jammed onto the end.

▲ Have a go at adding different colours to your text.

Both are used to display text in the window, but TextWindow.Write lets you keep writing on the same line as the previous text, whereas TextWindow.Writeline goes to a new line at the end.

Remember
- TextWindow displays just text

- TextWindow.Write adds text to the current line

- TextWindow.Writeline adds text to the current line, but the next output will be on the line below ●

BASIC ANALYSIS

```
TextWindow.WriteLine("Hello World")
```

You can see that your code can be split into three distinct sections: TextWindow calls the non-graphical text window object; WriteLine instructs the computer to display text; ("Hello World") gives the computer the words to display.

As software developers, we always have control over what the program does and how it looks, so let's have some fun with our text window. Modify your first program with the following code:

```
TextWindow.Title = "My First Program"
```

```
TextWindow.ForegroundColor = "Green"
```

```
TextWindow.WriteLine("I'm an awesome programmer!")
```

Execute your program with the Run button on the toolbar or F5 on the keyboard. Notice how your text window has changed from your first program because you've changed the properties of the text window object in the code. You now have a title at the top of the window and we have green text.

Sentence generator

Putting something on the screen is one thing, but programs also need to take some input from the user. We show you how

In our first basic project we learnt how to display a message to the user, but what if we need to ask the user for some information? Where do we store it and how do we use it? Handling input is a crucial part of programming, whether you're building a word processor or a paint package, or just a website with a form that needs to be filled in. We've already covered how you do this kind of thing in Scratch, but how do you do it in SmallBASIC?

It's easy. Type the following line of code in the editor window:

```
TextWindow.Write("Please enter your name: ")
```

```
name = TextWindow.Read()
```

```
TextWindow.Writeline("I'm very pleased to meet you " + name)
```

Now run the program. Notice how it waits until the user has entered a name before it continues with the rest of the code. This is because TextWindow.Read() pauses the program until the Enter key is pressed.

Storing information while our program is running is very important when we want to make more complex programs or have any interaction with the user. We call this storing variables. You might remember working with variables in Scratch. As in Scratch, a variable is a piece of data stored in memory, ready to be recalled by our code. Imagine we had a program that asked for the user's name, age and favourite sports team. If everyone gave the same answers, we could hardwire these answers into the code – we'd call these answers 'constants'. In real-life, however, everyone would give a

different set of answers. They'd vary, which is why we call them variables.

Working with numbers

Now that we've mastered text input, let's work with numbers. SmallBASIC has a built-in library of functions that we can call on to use in our own code. These save us precious time, as we don't have to fully code each function and define its purpose.

SmallBASIC has a math function that can perform a variety of maths tasks, such as dealing with degrees and radians, or even finding a number's square root. We're going to use one such function to get a random number.

Type the following code in the editor window:

```
RandomNumber=math.GetRandomNumber(49)
```

Now follow that up with another line:

```
TextWindow.Writeline("Your Random number is " + RandomNumber)
```

As you can see, we've concatenated our variable into a sentence, just as we did with the name earlier. Execute your program with Run or F5 and you can watch a random number get generated.

Making a sentence generator

We're going to combine both of our previous two examples to create a program that asks for the

BASIC ANALYSIS

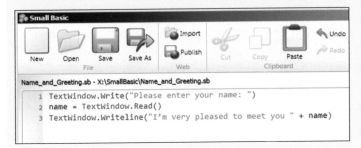

```
Name_and_Greeting.sb - X:\SmallBasic\Name_and_Greeting.sb
1  TextWindow.Write("Please enter your name: ")
2  name = TextWindow.Read()
3  TextWindow.Writeline("I'm very pleased to meet you " + name)
```

```
X:\SmallBasic\Name_and_Greeting.exe
Please enter your name: Mark Cox
I'm very pleased to meet you Mark Cox
Press any key to continue...
```

```
name = TextWindow.Read()
```

Take a close look at this instruction. Here, the TextWindow.Read() asks the computer to pause and wait for the user to type in something, then store it in memory as a variable called 'name'.

Now take a look at the final line of code: TextWindow.Writeline("I'm

very pleased to meet you " + name). Everyone gets the same greeting message. We're displaying our greeting message as normal, but then we recall the stored variable (name) and add it to the end, using the code '+ name'. This is called concatenation. Well done! You can now display text information on the screen as well as get information from a user.

user's name, then generates silly sentences by using random verbs and nouns. The trick to building a more complex program is to break down our problem into sections, and to make sure we get our events in the right order.

For our sentence denerator to work, we need the following events, in order.

1 Display a message asking for a name in a text window

2 Store that name in a variable

3 Generate and store a random verb from a list

4 Generate and store a random noun from a list

5 Display the user's name followed by the stored verb, then the stored noun in a text window.

OK. We're ready to start coding. Create a new page for the Code Editor and enter the following code:

```
TextWindow.Write("Please enter a name: ")
name = TextWindow.Read()
```

```
v=math.GetRandomNumber(4)

verb[1] = "walked "

verb[2] = "answered "

verb[3] = "danced "

verb[4] = "ate "

n=math.GetRandomNumber(4)

noun[1] = "the cake"

noun[2] = "the cat"

noun[3] = "the phone"

noun[4] = "the tango"

TextWindow.Writeline(name + " just " +
verb[v] + noun[n])
```

Run your code by pressing run on the toolbar or tapping F5.

The way we generate the variables for the verb and noun in this example is through a

TOP TIP
Planning out code and dividing it into a series of logical steps is an essential part of software development. We call this type of planning Pseudocode.

BASIC TRIVIA

Computers have to be told exactly what to do all the time, so asking them for a truly random number is actually more difficult than you might think. Some languages use the current clock speed of the CPU to determine the number, as it's constantly changing.

DIMENSIONS AND ARRAYS

An array that contains just one value is known as a single dimension array. There are more complex arrays that can have multiple values. These have a cool sci-fi name: a multi-dimensional array!

BASIC ANALYSIS

```
RandNumexample.sb * - X:\SmallBasic\RandNumexample.sb
1 RandomNumber=math.GetRandomNumber(49)
2 TextWindow.Writeline("Your Random number is " + RandomNumber)
```

```
X:\SmallBasic\RandNumexample.exe
Your Random number is 6
Press any key to continue...
```

`RandomNumber=math.GetRandomNumber(49)`

This code will generate a random number from 1 to 49 and assign it to a variable called RandomNumber. The math.GetRandomNumber

function works much like the Pick random operator block in Scratch. You can change the number in the brackets to any positive number, and it will then generate a random number from 1 to that maximum amount.

programming technique called an array. Using this method, you can have the same variable name followed by an index number to store multiple values. Remember the lists in Scratch? Those lists are really simple one-dimensional arrays. In this example, we generate a random number and match it to the index in the array. The syntax of an array is very straightforward in SmallBASIC:

`VariableName[number] = "Option"`

Don't forget to use square brackets with an array, not the usual rounded brackets that we use to display text.

We don't have to stop here. We can keep adding more words to the program's vocabulary by adding to the two verb and noun arrays. For example, we could add the following under our list of verbs:

SBSillySentence Code ext

`verb[5] = "jumped over "`

`verb[6] = "high-fived the "`

then the following to our list of nouns:

```
noun[5] = "the moon"
noun[6] = "the pandas"
```

All we'd have to do is change the figures in brackets after the two =math.GetRandomNumber instructions to the new total number of nouns or verbs, to read:

`n=math.GetRandomNumber(6)`

`v=math.GetRandomNumber(6)`

```
Small Basic
New  Open  Save  Save As  Import  Publish  Cut  Copy  Paste  Undo  Redo  Run (F5)  Grad
File              Web              Clipboard         Program
Untitled *
1 TextWindow.Write("Please enter a name: ")
2 name = TextWindow.Read()
3
4 v=math.GetRandomNumber(4)
5 verb[1] = "walked "
6 verb[2] = "answered "
7 verb[3] = "danced "
8 verb[4] = "ate "
9
10 n=math.GetRandomNumber(4)
11 noun[1] = "the cake"
12 noun[2] = "the cat"
13 noun[3] = "the phone"
14 noun[4] = "the tango"
15
16 TextWindow.Writeline(name + " just " + verb[v] + noun[n])
```

```
X:\SmallBasic\SentenceGen.exe
Please enter a name: James Rea
James Rea just walked the cat
Press any key to continue...
```

▲ Our program generates silly sentences by using random verbs and nouns.

Try changing the verbs and nouns in the list, or start adding a greater selection. Just don't forget to increase the maximum random number in brackets, and do so for the nouns and the verbs! ●

BASIC ANALYSIS

`TextWindow.Writeline(name + " just " + verb[v] + noun[n])`

Take a closer look at this instruction. Here, we're displaying the user's name stored at the start, followed by the word "just", then we're calling our verb with a random index number, and the same again with our noun. When we put all of the pieces in the correct order, we get a complete sentence, albeit a very silly one.

TOP TIP
Take care when giving your variables an assigned name. Don't start them with numbers or symbols like #Name or 99Name. It's often helpful to use several descriptive words joined together like FirstName or UserAge. This can make it much easier to understand and debug your program later on.

Create your own quiz

With a few simple instructions under our belt, we can now start to build
something more exciting. Let's kick off with a maths quiz

After the last few projects,
you should have enough
skills to start building
more complex programs,
but we need to experiment with
working with numbers, especially
addition, subtraction, multiplication
and division. With that in mind,
we're going to make a game that
manipulates numbers. As always,
before we start coding, we need to get
a clear idea of what we want to do and
the order in which it will happen.

Our first maths program is going to
follow this process:

1. Display game title in the text
window

2. Generate the first random number
between 1 and 100 and save that to
a variable

3. Generate the second random number between 1
and 100, and save that to a variable

4. Display the addition equation to the user in the
text window with both variables

5. Ask for an answer in the text window

6. Save their response into a variable

7. Check if the answer typed in matches the total
of the two numbers

8. Tell the user if they are correct or incorrect

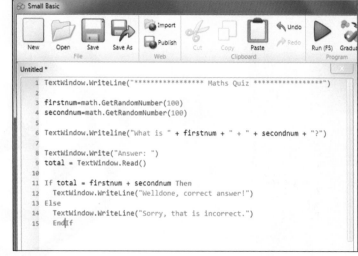

▲ Our maths quiz program uses a If statement to check whether the answer is
correct or not.

Begin the quiz
Start a new program and type in the following
code. When you're done, run the program with F5:

```
TextWindow.WriteLine("*****************
Maths Quiz *****************")

firstnum=math.GetRandomNumber(100)
secondnum=math.GetRandomNumber(100)

TextWindow.Writeline("What is " +
firstnum + " + " + secondnum + "?")

TextWindow.Write("Answer: ")
total = TextWindow.Read()

If total = firstnum + secondnum Then
```

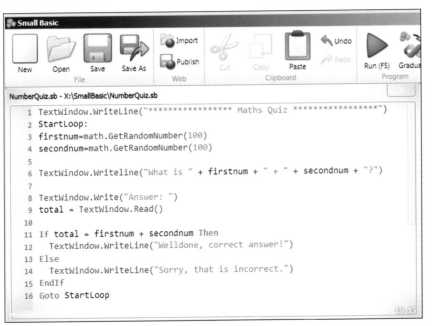

```
Small Basic
New   Open   Save   Save As    Import   Publish    Cut   Copy   Paste    Undo   Redo    Run (F5)  Gradu
      File                       Web              Clipboard                           Program

NumberQuiz.sb - X:\SmallBasic\NumberQuiz.sb

 1  TextWindow.WriteLine("**************** Maths Quiz ****************")
 2  StartLoop:
 3  firstnum=math.GetRandomNumber(100)
 4  secondnum=math.GetRandomNumber(100)
 5
 6  TextWindow.Writeline("What is " + firstnum + " + " + secondnum + "?")
 7
 8  TextWindow.Write("Answer: ")
 9  total = TextWindow.Read()
10
11  If total = firstnum + secondnum Then
12    TextWindow.WriteLine("Welldone, correct answer!")
13  Else
14    TextWindow.WriteLine("Sorry, that is incorrect.")
15  EndIf
16  Goto StartLoop
                                                            16, 15
```

```
X:\SmallBasic\NumberQuiz.exe
**************** Maths Quiz ****************
What is 41 + 93?
Answer: 134
Welldone, correct answer!
What is 2 + 82?
Answer: 84
Welldone, correct answer!
What is 78 + 90?
Answer: 168
Welldone, correct answer!
What is 80 + 64?
Answer: 144
Welldone, correct answer!
What is 42 + 77?
Answer: 5
Sorry, that is incorrect.
What is 22 + 98?
Answer:
```

```
  TextWindow.WriteLine("Welldone, correct
answer!")
Else
  TextWindow.WriteLine("Sorry, that is
incorrect.")
EndIf
```

▲ Loops in Small Basic work just like 'repeat' and 'forever' blocks in Scratch.

This program uses a conditional statement to check whether the answer is correct. If statements are used frequently in many programming languages to make choices and to interact with the user. In Small Basic, the structure of an If statement follows:

```
If condition Then
```

Code if the condition has been met

```
Else
```

Code if the condition has not been met

```
EndIf
```

Look at the If statement we've just typed in:

```
If total = firstnum + secondnum Then
  TextWindow.WriteLine("Welldone, correct
answer!")
Else
  TextWindow.WriteLine("Sorry, that is
incorrect.")
EndIf
```

Our condition in the statement was to check if the total variable is equal to the sum of the first and second variables, which gives us a true or false scenario that works well with mathematical equations, as they've either entered a correct or incorrect answer.

Using loops
One annoying problem we have with our program is that we only get one maths question before the program ends and we have to restart it. Wouldn't it be great if we could tell the computer to go back to the beginning of the code and ask another question automatically? Well, luckily Small Basic can do that by using a simple loop. Remember the 'repeat' and 'forever' blocks in Scratch? Loops work in exactly the same way.

Add the following code to line 2 within your existing program, just above generating the first random number and below the title:

```
StartLoop:
```

Add the following code to the very end of the code after the If statement block:

```
Goto StartLoop
```

What we've done is to create a marker at the top of the program called StartLoop. We can use any words we like for our marker, as long as they're joined together with no spaces and there's a colon at the end. When the code reaches Goto StartLoop at the end, it will head back to the top and rerun the code after our marker to repeat our code. Run your program again and you should get an infinite amount of questions, each one randomly generated.

So far, we've been working only with addition (+), but we can just as easily change this to subtraction, multiplication or division by altering the equation symbol in the first line of the If statement.

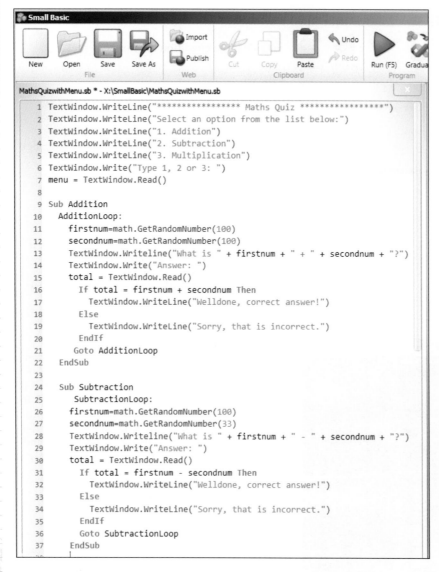

Small Basic

New · Open · Save · Save As · File · Import · Publish · Web · Cut · Copy · Paste · Clipboard · Undo · Redo · Run (F5) · Gradua · Program

MathsQuizwithMenu.sb * - X:\SmallBasic\MathsQuizwithMenu.sb

```
1  TextWindow.WriteLine("**************** Maths Quiz ****************")
2  TextWindow.WriteLine("Select an option from the list below:")
3  TextWindow.WriteLine("1. Addition")
4  TextWindow.WriteLine("2. Subtraction")
5  TextWindow.WriteLine("3. Multiplication")
6  TextWindow.Write("Type 1, 2 or 3: ")
7  menu = TextWindow.Read()
8
9  Sub Addition
10   AdditionLoop:
11     firstnum=math.GetRandomNumber(100)
12     secondnum=math.GetRandomNumber(100)
13     TextWindow.Writeline("What is " + firstnum + " + " + secondnum + "?")
14     TextWindow.Write("Answer: ")
15     total = TextWindow.Read()
16       If total = firstnum + secondnum Then
17         TextWindow.WriteLine("Welldone, correct answer!")
18       Else
19         TextWindow.WriteLine("Sorry, that is incorrect.")
20       EndIf
21     Goto AdditionLoop
22  EndSub
23
24  Sub Subtraction
25    SubtractionLoop:
26     firstnum=math.GetRandomNumber(100)
27     secondnum=math.GetRandomNumber(33)
28     TextWindow.Writeline("What is " + firstnum + " - " + secondnum + "?")
29     TextWindow.Write("Answer: ")
30     total = TextWindow.Read()
31       If total = firstnum - secondnum Then
32         TextWindow.WriteLine("Welldone, correct answer!")
33       Else
34         TextWindow.WriteLine("Sorry, that is incorrect.")
35       EndIf
36     Goto SubtractionLoop
37  EndSub
```

▲ Here, we've further developed our quiz using blocks of reusable code called subroutines.

To change your program to test subtraction:

```
If total = firstnum - secondnum Then
```

To change your program to test multiplication:

```
If total = firstnum * secondnum Then
```

To change your program to test division:

```
If total = firstnum / secondnum Then
```

EXPERIMENT

Try changing the maximum random number in the brackets to make your game harder or easier.

The only cosmetic change you'll need to make is where you display the equation to the user (line 6), as it will still have the addition symbol between the two numbers.

Just as if we were using spreadsheet software, the symbols for multiplication (*) and division (/) will differ to what you might be used to from your maths lessons at school. Multiplication is normally just an x symbol from the alphabet, but the computer needs the x to form different words, so we can't use that. There's also no standard division symbol on a keyboard, so we use the * and / symbols to represent them.

Developing the quiz

The great thing about programming is that once you have the basic code sorted out, you have a solid foundation on which to add extra features. Here, we need to give our program greater functionality by letting the user decide what area of arithmetic to practise, instead of having to change the source code manually. So, we're going to code a menu system, and the user can select which area of maths to improve.

Our new and improved maths quiz program is going to follow this process:

1 Display game title and menu options in the text window

2 Ask the user for their input

3 If the user selects Addition, call the subroutine code

4 If the user selects Multiplication, call the subroutine code

5 If the user selects Subtraction, call the subroutine code

The trick is to create reusable blocks of code called subroutines. These subroutine blocks will perform one of the arithmetic operations, such as a block for subtraction and one for multiplication, depending on what the user selects from the menu. If you remember the 'make' and 'define' blocks in Scratch, these effectively created subroutines that could be reused again and again. Creating a subroutine in Small Basic is very easy. You just need the Keyword sub followed by the name of your subroutine. Any code after this point will be part of that subroutine until you close it with EndSub. To call your subroutine, just use the name of it followed by two brackets: e.g. Addition ().

Modify your existing program or create a new one with the following code:

```
X:\SmallBasic\MathsQuizwithMenu.exe
****************** Maths Quiz ******************
Select an option from the list below:
1. Addition
2. Subtraction
3. Multiplication
Type 1, 2 or 3: 3
What is 3 * 9?
Answer: 27
Welldone, correct answer!
What is 3 * 3?
Answer: 9
Welldone, correct answer!
What is 4 * 7?
Answer: 28
Welldone, correct answer!
What is 2 * 5?
Answer: 5
Sorry, that is incorrect.
What is 9 * 3?
Answer:
```

▲ Our new and improved maths quiz program!

```
TextWindow.WriteLine("****************
Maths Quiz ******************")

TextWindow.WriteLine("Select an option
from the list below:")

TextWindow.WriteLine("1. Addition")

TextWindow.WriteLine("2. Subtraction")

TextWindow.WriteLine("3. Multiplication")

TextWindow.Write("Type 1, 2 or 3: ")
menu = TextWindow.Read()

Sub Addition
  AdditionLoop:
    firstnum=math.GetRandomNumber(100)
    secondnum=math.GetRandomNumber(100)
    TextWindow.Writeline("What is " +
firstnum + " + " + secondnum + "?")
    TextWindow.Write("Answer: ")
    total = TextWindow.Read()
    If total = firstnum + secondnum Then
       TextWindow.WriteLine("Welldone,
correct answer!")
       Else
       TextWindow.WriteLine("Sorry, that
is incorrect.")
      EndIf
    Goto AdditionLoop
  EndSub

  Sub Subtraction
    SubtractionLoop:
    firstnum=math.GetRandomNumber(100)
    secondnum=math.GetRandomNumber(33)
    TextWindow.Writeline("What is " +
firstnum + " - " + secondnum + "?")
    TextWindow.Write("Answer: ")
```

```
    total = TextWindow.Read()
    If total = firstnum - secondnum Then
       TextWindow.WriteLine("Welldone,
correct answer!")
       Else
       TextWindow.WriteLine("Sorry, that
is incorrect.")
      EndIf
    Goto SubtractionLoop
  EndSub

Sub Multiplication
  MultiplicationLoop:
    firstnum=math.GetRandomNumber(12)
    secondnum=math.GetRandomNumber(12)
    TextWindow.Writeline("What is " +
firstnum + " * " + secondnum + "?")
    TextWindow.Write("Answer: ")
    total = TextWindow.Read()
    If total = firstnum * secondnum Then
       TextWindow.WriteLine("Welldone,
correct answer!")
       Else
       TextWindow.WriteLine("Sorry, that
is incorrect.")
      EndIf
    Goto MultiplicationLoop
  EndSub

If menu = 1 Then
    Addition()
  Elseif menu = 2 Then
    Subtraction()
  Elseif menu = 3 Then
    Multiplication()
EndIf
```

Using Elseif

In Small Basic, we have to code all of the subroutines before we can call them – this is why the menu selection code is at the end of the program. You'll have also noticed that the If statement we're using now differs from the one we used in our first maths program, and we have a new keyword 'Elseif'. Because our menu has more than two possible options, we need to use Elseif to give us more conditional options. The syntax for using Elseif is very simple:

```
If condition1 then
```

CODING KEYWORDS

Subroutine: An independent block of code that can be recalled from within the main program.

> **TOP TIP**
> With more advanced subroutines, you can feed data, like variables, in and send data back out to the main program. The same subroutine can even be used by entirely different parts of a program, which is a lot more efficient than writing a new one every time you need it.

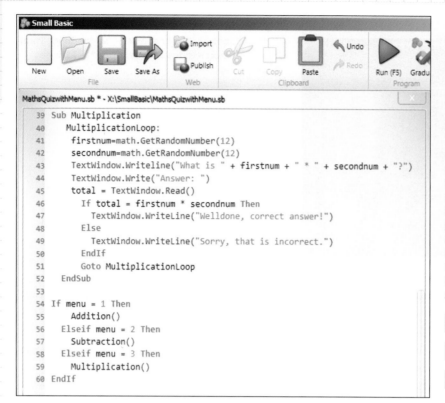

```
Small Basic

New    Open    Save    Save As    Import    Cut    Copy    Paste    Undo    Redo    Run (F5)  Gradu
                                    Publish
          File                        Web              Clipboard            Program

MathsQuizwithMenu.sb * - X:\SmallBasic\MathsQuizwithMenu.sb                        X

39  Sub Multiplication
40    MultiplicationLoop:
41      firstnum=math.GetRandomNumber(12)
42      secondnum=math.GetRandomNumber(12)
43      TextWindow.Writeline("What is " + firstnum + " * " + secondnum + "?")
44      TextWindow.Write("Answer: ")
45      total = TextWindow.Read()
46      If total = firstnum * secondnum Then
47        TextWindow.WriteLine("Welldone, correct answer!")
48      Else
49        TextWindow.WriteLine("Sorry, that is incorrect.")
50      EndIf
51      Goto MultiplicationLoop
52    EndSub
53
54  If menu = 1 Then
55    Addition()
56  Elseif menu = 2 Then
57    Subtraction()
58  Elseif menu = 3 Then
59    Multiplication()
60  EndIf
```

▲ Add as many Elseif statements as you like, depending on how many conditions you have to deal with.

```
Run this code

Elseif condition2 then

Run this code

Elseif condition3 then

Run this code

Else

Run this code

End if
```

TOP TIP

As subroutines are independent blocks of the code, the order in which you code them doesn't matter.

Now, we left the division element of the maths game out of our program so that you can have your first go at editing the program without having the solution. Think about all the aspects of the game so far, and you'll see that you need to add:

1. The new division option in the menu at the start

2. A subroutine for division. Don't forget to use the / symbol

3. A new Elseif option for the If statement at the end

You can add as many Elseif statements as you like, depending on how many conditions you have to deal with. The final statement is just an Else, as this is basically saying that if it's none of the above (condition1, condition2 or condition3) do the last piece of code in the list.

Adding a progress meter

The great thing about coding is that you can always add another feature. To make our program feel even more useful, we can add a progress tracker, so the user can see how many questions they've attempted, how many they've answered correctly and a percentage of their success. To do this, we're going to need three new variables: one to keep a count of how many questions have been asked (questions), one to keep track of correct responses (score) and one to calculate the percentage (percentage). To start with, add the following code above the first addition subroutine:

```
score = 0
```

```
questions = 0
```

```
percentage= 0
```

We need to amend each subroutine to include our score tracker, so let's start with the Addition subroutine. First, let's calculate how many questions we have correct: find our If statement that congratulates the user and just under that add the following code:

```
score = score + 1
```

This now means that after every correct question we're getting the current value of our variable score and moving it up by 1.

Now we need to keep track of how many questions have been asked so far by using our Questions variable. Add the following code underneath the If statement in our Addition subroutine:

```
questions = questions + 1
```

Again, just like our correct score counter, we're getting the value in the Questions variable and moving it up by 1.

If we have the number of questions correct and the total number of questions, we can calculate the percentage and keep that in a variable. Add the following code underneath our questions counter:

```
percentage = Math.Round((score /
questions) * 100)
```

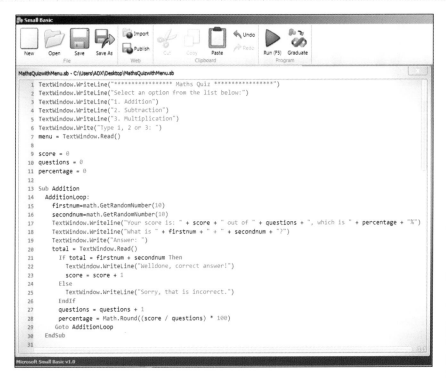

```
 1  TextWindow.WriteLine("************** Maths Quiz **************")
 2  TextWindow.WriteLine("Select an option from the list below:")
 3  TextWindow.WriteLine("1. Addition")
 4  TextWindow.WriteLine("2. Subtraction")
 5  TextWindow.WriteLine("3. Multiplication")
 6  TextWindow.Write("Type 1, 2 or 3: ")
 7  menu = TextWindow.Read()
 8
 9  score = 0
10  questions = 0
11  percentage = 0
12
13  Sub Addition
14    AdditionLoop:
15      firstnum=math.GetRandomNumber(10)
16      secondnum=math.GetRandomNumber(10)
17      TextWindow.Writeline("Your score is: " + score + " out of " + questions + ", which is " + percentage + "%")
18      TextWindow.Writeline("What is " + firstnum + " + " + secondnum + "?")
19      TextWindow.Write("Answer: ")
20      total = TextWindow.Read()
21      If total = firstnum + secondnum Then
22        TextWindow.WriteLine("Welldone, correct answer!")
23        score = score + 1
24      Else
25        TextWindow.WriteLine("Sorry, that is incorrect.")
26      EndIf
27      questions = questions + 1
28      percentage = Math.Round((score / questions) * 100)
29      Goto AdditionLoop
30  EndSub
31
```

In this line of code, we're first taking score and dividing it by questions, then multiplying by 100 to find the percentage number. We then take the result and store it in the variable called Percentage. We're also taking advantage of another built-in function in Small Basic: Math.Round. This gets our final number and rounds it either up or down. Lastly, display the score tracker with the percentage at the start of every question. Add this code underneath where we generated our random numbers:

▲ Test your program to make sure the score tracker is working for every subroutine.

```
TextWindow.Writeline("Your score is: " +
score + " out of " + questions + ", which
is " + percentage + "%")
```

BASIC ANALYSIS

```
percentage = Math.Round((score /
questions) * 100)
```

In this line of code, we've had to use a number of brackets. Math.Round needs a set of brackets that surround the entire equation, so that the number produced from the division gets rounded to a whole number. The brackets inside calculate the score divided by questions variable before it's multiplied by 100. In your maths lessons at school, you use BIDMAS (Brackets – Indices – Multiplication – Addition – Subtraction) to order the maths operation so you get the correct number. We follow the exact same rules when we're programming.

This code is basically a long line of variable concatenation that forms a complete sentence. It works in the same way as earlier in the program, when we displayed the questions with our random numbers in for the user. Don't forget normal text is just displayed within quotations marks (" "). We add in our variables by using the plus sign, variable name, then another plus sign, so add in the next piece (+ variablename +). The only time we don't need the final plus sign is when we're at the end of our sentence.

Our final addition subroutine should now look like the following, with the new code highlighted in red:

```
Sub Addition
  AdditionLoop:
    firstnum=math.GetRandomNumber(10)
    secondnum=math.GetRandomNumber(10)

    TextWindow.Writeline("Your score is:
" + score + " out of " + questions + ",
which is " + percentage + "%")

    TextWindow.Writeline("What is " +
firstnum + " + " + secondnum + "?")
    TextWindow.Write("Answer: ")
    total = TextWindow.Read()
    If total = firstnum + secondnum Then
      TextWindow.WriteLine("Welldone,
correct answer!")
      score = score + 1
    Else
      TextWindow.WriteLine("Sorry, that
is incorrect.")
    EndIf
    questions = questions + 1
    percentage = Math.Round((score /
questions) * 100)
    Goto AdditionLoop
  EndSub
```

Of course, to complete our full quiz, we're going to need to add those highlighted bits of code to the subtraction, multiplication and division subroutines in exactly the same place for each one. Remember to test your program to make sure the score tracker is working for every subroutine. ●

TAKE IT FURTHER

Try changing the program so that the user can select the difficulty of questions, which would be the highest values of your generated numbers. You can put variables in the random number brackets instead of numbers – math. GetRandomNumber(variablename)

Small Basic graphics

We've tangled with text and messed around with mathematics. Now it's time we got to grips with coding graphics

So far, we've been working exclusively with Small Basic's TextWindow object. However, when dealing with graphics, animation and drawing, we could call the GraphicsWindow.

Just like the TextWindow object, GraphicsWindow can be called into a program, and it has a number of properties we can modify. We can call shape outlines or filled shapes into the graphics window, including lines, rectangles, triangles and ellipses.

Try out the code below to see some of these shapes in action:

```
GraphicsWindow.Title = "Graphics"
```

```
GraphicsWindow.BackgroundColor =
"DarkBlue"
```

```
GraphicsWindow.Width = 200
```

```
GraphicsWindow.Height = 200
```

```
GraphicsWindow.PenWidth = 8
GraphicsWindow.PenColor = "LightBlue"
```

```
GraphicsWindow.DrawLine(10, 10, 10, 190)
```

CODING KEYWORDS

Arguments: Values that can be changed in properties of an object such as its position, height, width and colour. Programmers will usually refer to arguments as 'args'.

▲ This program shows you how to generate a random colour and create a rectangle with random coordinates, and more.

```
GraphicsWindow.PenWidth = 5
```

```
GraphicsWindow.DrawLine(22, 10, 22, 190)
```

```
GraphicsWindow.PenWidth = 2
```

```
GraphicsWindow.DrawLine(30, 10, 30, 190)
```

```
GraphicsWindow.PenColor = "Blue"
```

```
GraphicsWindow.FillEllipse(110, 110, 80,
80)
```

```
GraphicsWindow.DrawEllipse(40, 110, 80,
80)
```

```
GraphicsWindow.FillRectangle(40, 10, 70,
72)
```

```
GraphicsWindow.DrawRectangle(120, 10, 70,
70)
```

Drawing shapes in random locations

We can now add static shapes to our graphics window, but that's not very exciting, is it? Let's try to use the Small Basic code to make something less

BASIC ANALYSIS – DRAWING GRAPHICS

Just like with TextWindow object, we call the graphics object with GraphicsWindow, then define the type of shape, and whether it has a solid fill colour. The first two numbers in the brackets are the x and y pixel coordinates of the graphics window. To give you a point of reference: in a Small Basic graphics window that is 200 x 200 pixels, the top-left corner of the graphics window is coordinates 0,0 and the bottom right has the coordinates 200,200. The next two numbers after the coordinates in the brackets are the width and height of the shape in pixels.

Drawing lines and triangles is a slightly different process. The first two numbers for DrawLine are the x and y coordinates, which define where the start of the line should go. The last numbers are the x and y coordinates for the end of the line. The program then draws a straight line between those two points. When you call the triangle shape DrawTriangle you have six numbers in the brackets, as you have to provide x and y coordinates for each of the three points of the triangle.

Just as with our text colour, we can change the colour properties of our shapes, and will keep

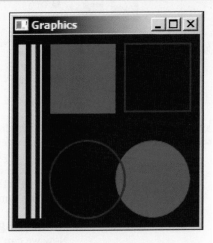

```
drawshapes.sb - X:\SmallBasic\drawshapes.sb
 1  GraphicsWindow.Title = "Graphics"
 2  GraphicsWindow.BackgroundColor = "DarkBlue"
 3  GraphicsWindow.Width = 200
 4  GraphicsWindow.Height = 200
 5
 6  GraphicsWindow.PenWidth = 8
 7  GraphicsWindow.PenColor = "LightBlue"
 8  GraphicsWindow.DrawLine(10, 10, 10, 190)
 9  GraphicsWindow.PenWidth = 5
10  GraphicsWindow.DrawLine(22, 10, 22, 190)
11  GraphicsWindow.PenWidth = 2
12  GraphicsWindow.DrawLine(30, 10, 30, 190)
13
14  GraphicsWindow.PenColor = "Blue"
15  GraphicsWindow.FillEllipse(110, 110, 80, 80)
16  GraphicsWindow.DrawEllipse(40, 110, 80, 80)
17
18  GraphicsWindow.FillRectangle(40, 10, 70, 72)
19  GraphicsWindow.DrawRectangle(120, 10, 70, 70)
```

that colour until it's changed later in the code:

```
GraphicsWindow.PenColor =
"Magenta"
```

When drawing lines, you can specify how thick the line can be using the following line of code before the drawing the line, and again it will keep that thickness until it's given another value:

```
GraphicsWindow.PenWidth = 2
```

We can now start to tell our program the width and height of our graphics window in pixels, using the following code:

```
GraphicsWindow.Width = 200
```

```
GraphicsWindow.Height = 200
```

predictable. Our next program is going to follow this sequence:

1 Set the background colour to black

2 Start a loop marker

3 Generate a random colour

4 Generate a random number (max 640) and assign it to a variable called x

5 Generate a random number (max 480) and assign it to a variable called y

6 Create a rectangle (20 x 20) with the random x and y coordinates

7 Loop back around to the start of the loop marker

▲ Our program in action!

Create a new code window and add the following code.

```
GraphicsWindow.BackgroundColor = "Black"
StartLoop:

GraphicsWindow.BrushColor =

GraphicsWindow.GetRandomColor()

x = Math.GetRandomNumber(640)

y = Math.GetRandomNumber(480)

GraphicsWindow.FillRectangle(x, y, 20,
20)

Program.Delay(100)

Goto StartLoop
```

Just before the end of the code, we've added a new feature called Program.Delay(100), which will pause the program before it loops around, giving us the ability to change the speed in which the program runs. The length of that pause can be changed with the number in brackets, which represents time in milliseconds: try making that

EXPERIMENT

Try adding your own shapes to get used to how the coordinate system works. If you get stuck, change just one number in the brackets and see what effect that has on the shape or its position in the GraphicsWindow.

```
1 MySquare = Shapes.AddRectangle(100, 100)
2 Shapes.Animate(MySquare, 530, 0, 3000)
```

▲ Have a go at animating a square across the screen.

number higher and lower from its value of 100 and see what effect that has on the program.

Another good experiment with this program is to change the size of the rectangle from 20, 20 to values higher or lower, but you'll need to keep them the same if you want a perfect square.

Animating shapes

Now we can try to animate a square across the screen by using some new code keywords, Shape.AddRectangle and Shape.Animate.

Quickly test the following code in a new window:

```
MySquare = Shapes.AddRectangle(100, 100)
Shapes.Animate(MySquare, 530, 0, 3000)
```

We're defining the shape called MySquare, just like we would a variable, and giving it a rectangle that is 100 x 100 in width and height. Now that we have a shape name defined, we can use Shapes.Animate to move MySquare from its starting 0,0 coordinate to 530,0 coordinate over a time span of 3,000 milliseconds.

Make a snow globe simulator

For our final graphics program, we're going to create a snow globe simulator, in which we can change the variables to switch between a gentle snowstorm or a raging blizzard. The mechanics of the program are simple: we're creating an array of ellipses off screen at the top, and randomising the start and end position. We can then use variables to control how our simulator works, changing the speed, size and density of the snowflakes.

Create a new code window and add the following code:

```
GraphicsWindow.BackgroundColor = "Black"

GraphicsWindow.BrushColor = "White"

GraphicsWindow.fillEllipse(300, 400, 75,
75)

GraphicsWindow.fillEllipse(315, 370, 45,
45)

GraphicsWindow.BrushColor = "black"

GraphicsWindow.fillEllipse(322, 380, 10,
10)

GraphicsWindow.fillEllipse(340, 380, 10,
10)

flakesize = 7
flakespeed = 3000
flakedensity = 50
rows = 20
columns = 20

For r = 1 To rows
  For c = 1 To columns
    startpos = Math.GetRandomNumber(700)
    opacity = Math.GetRandomNumber(120)
    GraphicsWindow.BrushColor = "White"
    snow[r][c] = Shapes.
AddEllipse(flakesize, flakesize)
    Shapes.SetOpacity(snow[r][c],
opacity)
Shapes.Move(snow[r][c], startpos, -30)
  EndFor
EndFor
```

BASIC ANALYSIS

```
Shapes.Animate(MySquare, 530, 0 , 3000)
```

We call our animation function with Shapes.Animate. Our first argument in brackets is the name of the shape – MySquare. Next, we have to give coordinate locations of where the shape will finish (530,0) followed by how long the animation will take in milliseconds (3000).

GO FURTHER

Instead of squares, try changing the code so that it produces ellipses or triangles. While you're at it, see if you can modify the program so the rectangles that appear each time are random sizes. Have a look at how we've used our x and y variables for the shape position to help you.

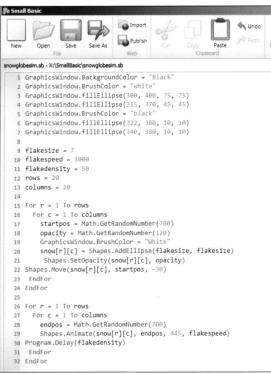

```
snowglobesim.sb - X:\SmallBasic\snowglobesim.sb
 1  GraphicsWindow.BackgroundColor = "Black"
 2  GraphicsWindow.BrushColor = "white"
 3  GraphicsWindow.fillEllipse(300, 400, 75, 75)
 4  GraphicsWindow.fillEllipse(315, 370, 45, 45)
 5  GraphicsWindow.BrushColor = "black"
 6  GraphicsWindow.fillEllipse(322, 380, 10, 10)
 7  GraphicsWindow.fillEllipse(340, 380, 10, 10)
 8
 9  flakesize = 7
10  flakespeed = 3000
11  flakedensity = 50
12  rows = 20
13  columns = 20
14
15  For r = 1 To rows
16    For c = 1 To columns
17      startpos = Math.GetRandomNumber(700)
18      opacity = Math.GetRandomNumber(120)
19      GraphicsWindow.BrushColor = "White"
20      snow[r][c] = Shapes.AddEllipse(flakesize, flakesize)
21      Shapes.SetOpacity(snow[r][c], opacity)
22  Shapes.Move(snow[r][c], startpos, -30)
23    EndFor
24  EndFor
25
26  For r = 1 To rows
27    For c = 1 To columns
28      endpos = Math.GetRandomNumber(700)
29      Shapes.Animate(snow[r][c], endpos, 445, flakespeed)
30  Program.Delay(flakedensity)
31    EndFor
32  EndFor
```

▶ Here's our snowman enjoying a gentle snowstorm!

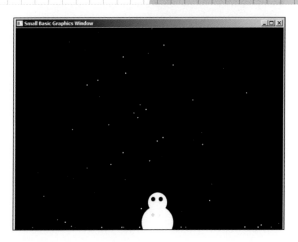

◀ The mechanics of the snow globe simulator are actually pretty simple.

```
For r = 1 To rows
  For c = 1 To columns
    endpos = Math.GetRandomNumber(700)
    Shapes.Animate(snow[r][c], endpos,
445, flakespeed)
Program.Delay(flakedensity)
  EndFor
EndFor
```

This program uses the For loop, which repeats a block of code a certain number of times using a counter. When the counter reaches the predetermined value – which can be a variable value – the loop will stop and return to running the main program. The syntax for the For loop is simple:

```
For condition
code to loop
EndFor
```

As this is a simulator, you can change the variable numbers and see what happens within the globe. Change the following variable for the size of each virtual snowflake (ellipse):

```
flakesize = 7
```

The following variable is put into the Delay function at the end; the lower the number (milliseconds), the more snowflakes will be released simultaneously:

```
flakedensity = 80
```

The next variable is the speed at which each snowflake will fall from the start to the end of its run. Remember, the number is in milliseconds so the lower you go, the faster the snow will fall:

```
flakespeed = 3000
```

To make our snow more realistic, we're using the code SetOpacity, which will work from random numbers, 0 being invisible and 100 being completely visible. This means that each square or virtual snowflake that's created will have a random transparency value, so some snowflakes are more visible than others, giving the illusion of depth and size. You could set this number higher than 100 as we've done, because then there's a greater probability of generating higher numbers, although anything generated over 100 will still be treated as 100. ●

CODING KEYWORDS

Syntax: The structure and order of the code in a program. Syntax is a vital part of any textual programming language. Ignore syntax, and your program won't run.

EXPERIMENT

Try putting Program.Delay(3000) after the last Shapes. Animate code, then try moving it to another coordinate location with another line of animation. See if you can make the square move around the perimeter of the graphics window with a delay separating each line of new animate code.

GOAL

Chapter

4

TOOLBOX

Section 4
The next level

With the help of SmallBASIC, we've learnt to put together simple BASIC programs. Yet while SmallBASIC is a surprisingly powerful and easy-to-learn implementation of the language, there will come a time when you'll need something more flexible, and with more built-in features. That's where Visual Basic comes in.

For the next few projects, we'll be using a free version of a proper programming environment – the same tools used by millions of professional software developers every day. That means you'll have to cope with a little more complexity, but you'll soon find that it isn't as hard as it first looks.

By the end of this chapter, you'll have some serious coding skills. The only question is, where will you take them next?

IN THIS SECTION

Introducing Visual Basic

SmallBASIC can take you a long way on your coding journey, but eventually you'll want a little more power. That's where Visual Basic comes in

- About VB, and how to get it for free

- How to work with buttons, forms and code

- How to code a simple control panel

Visual Basic is part of Microsoft's Visual Studio, an IDE (Integrated Development Environment) suite of programming tools that lets you work with a variety of coding languages, including C++, C# and Visual Basic. The full professional package doesn't come cheap, but there's a free edition, Visual Studio Express 2013 for Desktop, which gives you access to a still very powerful set of tools and built-in functions, with which you can build almost any kind of program, game or app. The latest 2013 version requires you to sign up for a Microsoft account, which you'll need to do in order to use the free version after the 30-day trial period is up.

Where can you find it?
There are several versions of Visual Studio, so make sure you search for the free version – Visual Studio Express 2013 for Desktop – rather than the high-end professional versions. You can find it at www.visualstudio.com/downloads/download-visual-studio-vs#d-express-windows-desktop

The Visual Studio website also has a variety of guides and documentation, covering everything from setting up the software to developing applications. You can find these at www.visualstudio.com/get-started/overview-of-get-started-tasks-vs

How can I use it?
Unlike Scratch or SmallBASIC, Visual Studio is a professional piece of software that you'd use as a professional developer for the Windows platform. The free version that you'll install will look nearly identical to the full version, so when you first start using it the menus and buttons may seem daunting. Don't worry. We're going to guide you through all the sections that you'll need to use at first.

As Visual Studio itself covers a variety of languages and can be used for many different Windows applications, when you first create a new application it will ask you what type of program you're going to create. For all the examples in the book, we'll choose the most common application type, which is a Windows Forms Application.

The code for Visual Basic isn't a million miles away from the code you might use for SmallBASIC, but now we have full control over our interface. We can design and draw buttons, forms, textboxes, and label boxes with our mouse before we type any code. All of these visual components are located in

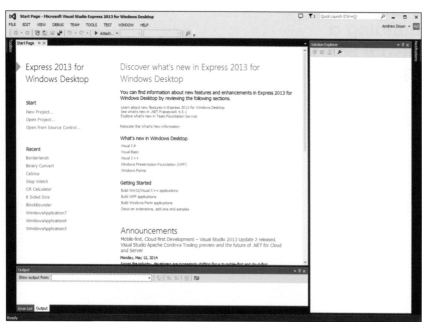

◀ There are several versions of Visual Studio, so make sure you search for the free version.

"The code for Visual Basic isn't a million miles away from the code for SmallBASIC"

a toolbox on the left of the screen. You can either scroll through these or search for a pre-made object and drag it onto the form.

Visual Basic is an event-driven language, so when we're ready to add code we double-click on an object, such as a button, then add the code that works behind that button. Your Visual Studio environment will try to help you code by guessing what you're about to type. We call this 'Intellisense'. It works a bit like predictive texting on mobile phones, but the computer knows the language keywords and every property, so you can use Enter or space on the keyboard to automatically complete the words you're typing.

What is Solution Explorer?

Many of the options we're going to change when designing the GUI in Visual Basic will be through

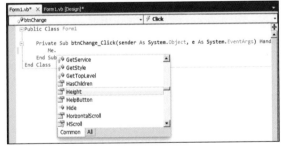

▲ Intellisense works a bit like predictive texting on mobile phones, automatically completing words you type.

NAMING BASICS

Naming your forms and controls is important, both because you want to make your code understandable and because you'll have to reference them in the code by their name. In order to remember what Button1, Button2 and Button 3 are, we'll give them descriptive names. A method developers use to start a name is to shorten the type of the control or form down to three letters first, followed by a descriptive name without any spaces:

Buttons – btnStart   Textbox – txtPlayerName
Labels – lblPlayerScore   Forms – frmMainGame

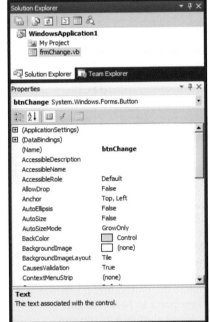

◄ All of the visual components are located in the toolbox.

the Properties window on the left of the screen. This menu will change depending on what item is selected. Also, above the Properties window you'll see the Solution Explorer: this will tell you the names of your documents and resources, as well as what forms you've created inside the current project.

Just like SmallBASIC, programs are executed with the Run button at the top of the page. This gets the computer to compile your code and creates an EXE file. If there are any problems or bugs, you'll get a report at the bottom of the screen. As Visual Basic is a more complex language, you're more likely to, and the help you get on any problems can use some quite technical wording. Luckily, the internet can help. If you get stuck with an error, try typing it into Google or Bing, and you'll often find some other programmers talking about the issue.

Our first Visual Basic app

To get familiar with the IDE and the programming language, we're going to create a simple app that allows the user to change the colour and dimensions of a form and its buttons, as well as add a counter and hide the buttons.

Start Visual Studio and create a new Windows Forms Application. Change the name of the project to ControlPanel and click OK. You'll get the default form (300 x 300 pixels), which can be resized. Drag the lower-left corner out so we have more room to add controls. With the form selected, have a look through the Property window on the right of the screen. This menu will show all the properties (name, colours, appearance, etc) of our form, and we can change and customise all of the values. Scroll through your list and find the Name

▲ Many of the options we're going to change when designing the GUI in Visual Basic will be through the Properties window.

▲ If there are any problems or bugs, you'll get a report at the bottom of the screen.

property, and change this to frmControlPanel.

To add buttons to our form, we need to look through the Visual Basic toolbox located on the left of the screen, which has a list of pre-made controls that we can drag to our form; by default, it will be called Button1. Find the control Button in the list and either double-click to automatically

▶ Start Visual Studio and create a new Windows Forms Application.

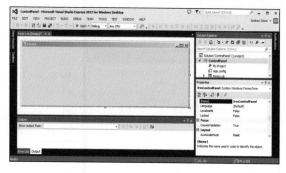

▶ Find the Name property, and change this to frmControlPanel.

draw the button to the form, or single-click and manually drag the size of button you want. Your first action after adding a new control is to rename it to btnHeightMax. Before then, change the Text property (the wording on the button) to Form Height +. Next, create another button next to your first one and rename the button btnHeightMin and change the Text property to Form Height -.

We're now ready to start adding our first piece of code. Double-click your first button btnHeightMax and you'll be taken to Code view, where Visual Studio has already put in all the

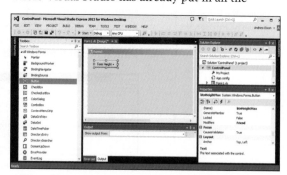

▲ After adding a new control, rename it to btnHeightMax.

required code to make a subroutine. Don't change or delete any of this code, as this will probably result in an error that you may not be able to fix.

We're going place our code in the middle of the Button subroutine, which you can find after the Private Sub line and before the End Sub line. We want our button to increase the height of our form by 10 pixels with the following line of code:

```
Me.Height = Me.Height + 10
```

At the top of the page, you'll now have two tabs with your Form name, so you can switch between the form design and our Code view. Try switching between the two now, so you know how to get from one to the other.

Double-click the btnHeightMin button on the form, and Visual Studio will again add the initial subroutine code. Just add the following code in between the Private Sub line and the End Sub line:

```
Me.Height = Me.Height - 10
```

▲ Place your code in the middle of the Button subroutine.

To test that our program works so far, we can compile and execute it using the green Play button at the top of the page, or by pressing F5. Try your btnHeightMax button and see if every click increases the height by 10 pixels, then test your btnHeightMin button to see if it does the opposite. You won't be able to make any changes to your form or code while the program is running, so close it with the Stop button, next to the Play button.

BASIC ANALYSIS

```
Me.height = Me.height + 10
```

As in SmallBASIC, we refer to the object first, then use a full stop and refer to its property. In Visual Basic, we can't directly refer to the name of the form that we're currently using, so we use the word: Me. Our code is instructing the computer to get the box's current height in pixels and add 10 to that number.

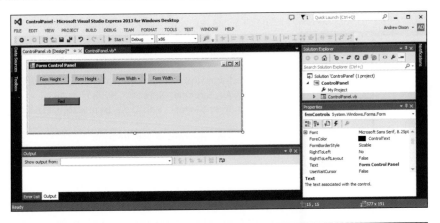

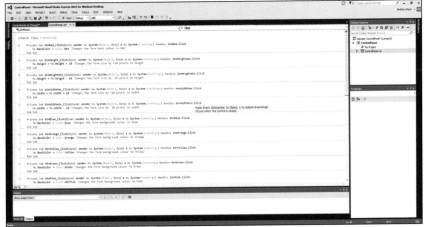

▲ Create a selection of other colours, which the user can decide to change to.

You have all the skills now to add two more buttons that will increase and decrease the width of the form. The code will nearly be identical; just remember to change the width not the height.

Changing colours

Now we're going to spice things up by giving our form colour themes. Create a new button called btnRed and change the display text to say Red. To emphasise that this button is going to change something to red, we can make the actual button red by changing BackColor open to red in the Property window. When you're ready to add the

◀ To emphasise that this button is going to change something to red, we can make the actual button red.

code, double-click the red button and type the following statement:

`Me.BackColor = Color.Red`

Run your program again and see what effect your red button has!

Repeat the task we've just completed with the red button to create a selection of other colours, which the user can decide to change to. Each time, rename the button, change the displayed text and manually change the button colour to match the colour it will be in the code. Arrange your buttons in a logical order and add a groupbox from the Toolbox menu, which can be drawn around your buttons to give them a separated border. Then, change the text to Colour Palette.

Adding a Reset button

We're going to add a Reset button to our form, which will revert all of our dimensions back to the state when you first started the program, and we'll set the colour back to the starting grey, so it will look like we've just restarted the entire program. Add a button onto your form and call it btnReset and change the display text to Reset. You can change the style and size if you wish:

`Me.Height = 191`

`Me.Width = 577`

`Me.BackColor = Color.LightGray`

The size of our form will differ from yours, so click on your form in Design view and have a look down the Property menu for Size. You'll see two numbers separated by a comma. This is the width and height in pixels; use those numbers in the code not ours for Me.Width and Me.Height.

Most visible toolbox controls such as buttons, textboxes and labels have a visibility property that we can change in the code as a Boolean value. Create two new buttons called btnVisible and btnInvisible, give their button text an appropriate name, then position them by your Reset button, as this will hide or show this button. The code for the invisible button will be:

`btnReset.Visible = False`

The code of the visible button will be the same; just reverse the Boolean value:

`btnReset.Visible = True`

▲ Our counter, when clicked, will increase a number in a label box, and another button to decrease the number.

Adding a counter

The last feature to add to our control panel is a counter, which when clicked will increase a number in a label box, and another button to decrease the number. For this, we're going to need three controls. Place two buttons on the form called btnCountUp and btnCountDown, and for the display text insert a + for one and a – for the other. Don't forget fonts and sizes can be found in the Property menu under Font. In between the two numbers, have a label box called lblCounter and set the display text to 0.

The code for our btnCountUp button is:

```
lblCounter.Text = lblCounter.Text + 1
```

The code for our btnCountDown button is:

```
lblCounter.Text = lblCounter.Text - 1
```

Give your program a test to see if all buttons on the page work as you want them to, either by pressing F5 or clicking the Run button at the top of the page. Save your program so you can see how you've written the code, in case you want to revisit it in the future to expand some new ideas.

Final code

```
Public Class frmControls

    Private Sub btnRed_Click(ByVal sender
As System.Object, ByVal e As System.
EventArgs) Handles btnRed.Click
        Me.BackColor = Color.Red 'Changes
the form back colour to RED
    End Sub

    Private Sub btnHeight_Click(ByVal
sender As System.Object, ByVal e As
System.EventArgs) Handles btnHeightmax.
Click
```

```
        Me.Height += +10 'Changes the
form size by +10 pixels in height
    End Sub

    Private Sub btnHeightmin_Click(ByVal
sender As System.Object, ByVal e As
System.EventArgs) Handles btnHeightmin.
Click
        Me.Height = Me.Height - 10
'Changes the form size by -10 pixels in
height
    End Sub

    Private Sub btnWidthMax_Click(ByVal
sender As System.Object, ByVal e As
System.EventArgs) Handles btnWidthMax.
Click
        Me.Width = Me.Width + 10 'Changes
the form size by +10 pixels in width
    End Sub

    Private Sub btnWidthmin_Click(ByVal
sender As System.Object, ByVal e As
System.EventArgs) Handles btnWidthmin.
Click
        Me.Width = Me.Width - 10 'Changes
the form size by -10 pixels in width
    End Sub

    Private Sub btnBlue_Click(ByVal
sender As System.Object, ByVal e As
System.EventArgs) Handles btnBlue.Click
        Me.BackColor = Color.Blue
'Changes the form background colour to
blue
    End Sub

    Private Sub btnOrange_Click(ByVal
sender As System.Object, ByVal e As
System.EventArgs) Handles btnOrange.Click
        Me.BackColor = Color.Orange
'Changes the form background colour to
Orange
    End Sub

    Private Sub btnYellow_Click(ByVal
sender As System.Object, ByVal e As
System.EventArgs) Handles btnYellow.Click
        Me.BackColor = Color.Yellow
'Changes the form background colour to
Yellow
```

CODING KEYWORDS

Boolean: A type of data that can only exist in one state – True – or another – False.

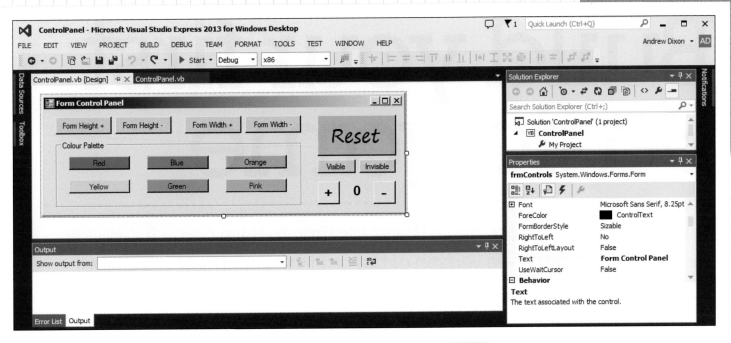

```
    End Sub

    Private Sub btnGreen_Click(ByVal
sender As System.Object, ByVal e As
System.EventArgs) Handles btnGreen.Click
        Me.BackColor = Color.Green
'Changes the form background colour to
Green
    End Sub

    Private Sub btnPink_Click(ByVal
sender As System.Object, ByVal e As
System.EventArgs) Handles btnPink.Click
        Me.BackColor = Color.HotPink
'Changes the form background colour to
Pink
    End Sub

    Private Sub btnReset_Click(ByVal
sender As System.Object, ByVal e As
System.EventArgs) Handles btnReset.Click
        Me.Height = 191 'Sets the height
back to 191 pixels
        Me.Width = 577 'sets the width
back to 577 pixels
        Me.BackColor = Color.LightGray
'Sets the colour back to the original
grey
        lblCounter.Text = 0 'Resets the
counter back to 0
    End Sub

    Private Sub btnVisible_Click(ByVal
sender As System.Object, ByVal e As
System.EventArgs) Handles btnVisible.
```

▲ Give your program a test to
see if all buttons on the page
work as you want them to.

```
Click
        btnReset.Visible = True 'Makes
the Reset button visible
    End Sub

    Private Sub Button1_Click(ByVal
sender As System.Object, ByVal e As
System.EventArgs) Handles Button1.Click
        btnReset.Visible = False 'Makes
the Reset button invisible
    End Sub

    Private Sub btnCountUp_Click(ByVal
sender As System.Object, ByVal e As
System.EventArgs) Handles btnCountUp.
Click
        lblCounter.Text = lblCounter.Text
+ 1 'Increases the lblCounter number by 1
    End Sub

    Private Sub btnCountDown_Click(ByVal
sender As System.Object, ByVal e As
System.
EventArgs) Handles btnCountDown.Click
        lblCounter.Text = lblCounter.Text
- 1 'Decreases the lblCounter number by 1
    End Sub
End Class
```

TOP TIP
When you've
completed a working
program, high-five
the nearest human
being!

EXPERIMENT

Can you add a line of code to btnReset so that the text
of lblCounter is set back to 0?

Build your first Basic game

Now you've got a feel for Visual Basic, it's time to have some fun building our first simple game – a version of the original blockbuster Breakout

> How to use PictureBoxes to create elements for a game

> How to move objects around the screen

> How to detect when objects collide

> How to use private variables

> How to use subroutines to make your programs more efficient

The first game we're going to create in Visual Basic is a version of the pioneering arcade favourite, Breakout. The player controls a bat that has to deflect a ball around the arena, hitting all the blocks without letting the ball slip behind them. Points are scored for each block you hit, and you need to hit all the blocks to clear the level; if you hit the floor too many times, the game will end. It's one of the oldest and simplest arcade games, and one developers still come back to for inspiration today. Putting it together is reasonably straightforward.

Create a new Window Forms Applications project, and give it a cool-sounding name for the game's title like 'Oblong Offensive'. Our first task is to resize the form so that we have a bigger arena to

bounce the ball. So with the form selected, change the size value in the Property window to 1000, 760, as this is the length and width in pixels.

While we have the Property window open, change the Name value to the title of the form name to 'Oblong Offensive' in the Name field.

Adding walls

We now need to add walls to each side of the arena so the ball can bounce off each one. For each wall, we're going to use the PictureBox control from the toolbox, which is great for inserting images or filling them with colours. Drag a PictureBox onto the form and resize it to the length of the form, then place it at the top of the screen. Change the name of the PictureBox to pctWallTop, then the colour using both the Name and Backcolor values in the Property window.

Now create another PictureBox, rename it pctWallBottom, give it a colour, then position it at the bottom of the page. Next, create a third PictureBox, rename it pctWallLeft, give it a colour and position it on the left of the page. Finally, create a fourth PictureBox, rename it pctWallRight, give it a colour and position it at the right of the page.

We now need to add the ball. Again, this is going to be a PictureBox called pctBall, but this time change the size to equal width and height (18, 18) by changing the Size property.

Getting the ball moving

It's time to get our ball moving around the screen and bouncing off each of the four walls, so we'll need a Timer control from the toolbox. Drag one from the toolbox onto our form (this will appear underneath) and rename it tmrMovement. We're also going to set the interval value in the property window to 25. Double-clicking the tmrMovement

Design	
(Name)	**OblongOffensive**
Language	(Default)
Localizable	False
Locked	False
Focus	
CausesValidation	True
Layout	
AutoScaleMode	**Font**
AutoScroll	False
⊞ AutoScrollMargin	0, 0
⊞ AutoScrollMinSize	0, 0
AutoSize	False
AutoSizeMode	GrowOnly
⊞ Location	0, 0
⊞ MaximumSize	0, 0
⊞ MinimumSize	0, 0
⊞ Padding	0, 0, 0, 0
⊞ Size	**1000, 760**
StartPosition	WindowsDefaultLocation
WindowState	Normal

▶ Change the size value in the Property window to 1000, 760.

FIND THE RIGHT DIRECTION

This handy table shows how we need to set the variables if we want to move the ball's vertical and horizontal pixel location, so that it goes where we want it to on screen. If you want to test if the direction is working, you can manually change isBallRight and isBallUp to either true or false in the code below. Just watch out: it won't bounce yet!

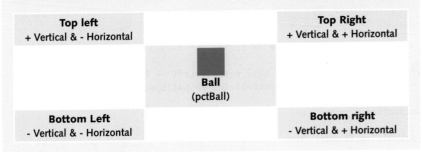

Top left		Top Right
+ Vertical & - Horizontal		+ Vertical & + Horizontal
	Ball (pctBall)	
Bottom Left		Bottom right
- Vertical & - Horizontal		- Vertical & + Horizontal

icon under the form will take us through to the Code view.

We're going to need some variables to set both the horizontal and vertical speed of our ball

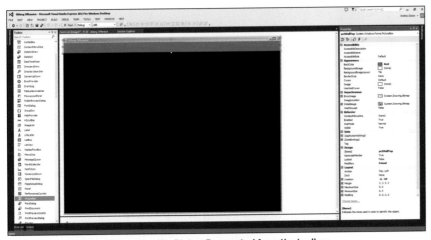

▲ For each wall, we're going to use the PictureBox control from the toolbox.

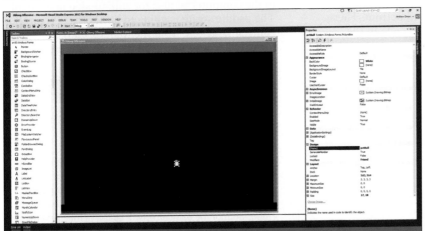

▲ To add the ball, create a PictureBox called pctBall.

> ❝ For each wall, we're going to use the PictureBox control from the toolbox ❞

(pctBall), as well as variables for which direction it will be moving in. Just above the tmrMovement subroutine that we've created, and underneath the name of our Class, we can insert our global variables that all subroutines can access. Enter the following variables:

```
Dim isBallRight As Boolean = True

Dim isBallUp As Boolean = False

Dim ballSpeedVertical As Integer = 3

Dim ballSpeedHorizontal As Integer = 3
```

To check what direction our ball is moving in, we're going to have two Boolean variables called isBallRight and isBallUp. As you might remember, a Boolean can have only two states: either true or false. The variable isBallRight = True will flag that the ball should be going right. If it's false, we can assume the opposite, to indicate the ball should be travelling left. The same is true of the isBallUp variable, because if it equals true it will signify an upward movement, and a false value will be the opposite downwards movement. The last two variables are going to regulate the speed of our ball (pctBall) on both the horizontal and vertical plane.

Visual Basic can move objects around in the window by increasing or decreasing their position by pixels. Because the ball is in a Timer control, it will keep moving. If you look at a flight of stairs in a house from a side angle, the shape of it will go slightly across then up, then across and up, then across and up, etc. This is exactly how our ball shape will move, changing the horizontal pixels followed by the vertical pixels. Since this happens so fast, it will appear that the ball is moving smoothly in all four diagonal directions.

We now need to get our ball moving by assigning each possible combination of our Boolean value variables to the corresponding horizontal and vertical speed in the tmrMovement subroutine:

```
If isBallRight = True Then pctBall.Left
```

```
Form1.vb ⇄ × Form1.vb [Design]

OblongOffensive                                                    ▼  ▦ (Declarations)

⊟ Public Class OblongOffensive

        Dim isBallRight As Boolean = True
        Dim isBallUp As Boolean = False
        Dim ballSpeedVertical As Integer = 3
        Dim ballSpeedHorizontal As Integer = 3

⊟       Private Sub tmrMovement_Tick(ByVal sender As System.Object, ByVal e As System.EventArgs) Handles tmrMovement.Tick

            If isBallRight = True Then pctBall.Left += ballSpeedHorizontal Else pctBall.Left -= ballSpeedHorizontal
            If isBallUp = True Then pctBall.Top -= ballSpeedVertical Else pctBall.Top += ballSpeedVertical

            If pctBall.Bounds.IntersectsWith(pctWallBottom.Bounds) Then
                isBallUp = True
            ElseIf pctBall.Bounds.IntersectsWith(pctWallTop.Bounds) Then
                isBallUp = False
            End If

            If pctBall.Bounds.IntersectsWith(pctWallLeft.Bounds) Then
                isBallRight = True
            ElseIf pctBall.Bounds.IntersectsWith(pctWallRight.Bounds) Then
                isBallRight = False
            End If

        End Sub
```

▲ We're using variables to set both the horizontal and vertical speed of our ball.

```
+= ballSpeedHorizontal Else pctBall.Left
-= ballSpeedHorizontal
```

```
If isBallUp = True Then pctBall.Top -=
ballSpeedVertical Else pctBall.Top +=
ballSpeedVertical
```

We use the .Left and .Top property of the PictureBox to give us the horizontal and vertical plane.

Making the ball bounce

To make our ball bounce around the arena, we're going to create an If statement for left and right, and one for top and bottom. These can go under the last piece of code in the tmrMovement subroutine:

```
If pctBall.Bounds.
IntersectsWith(pctWallBottom.Bounds) Then
            isBallUp = True
    ElseIf pctBall.Bounds.
IntersectsWith(pctWallTop.Bounds) Then
            isBallUp = False
End If
```

```
If pctBall.Bounds.
IntersectsWith(pctWallLeft.Bounds) Then
            isBallRight = True
    ElseIf pctBall.Bounds.
IntersectsWith(pctWallRight.Bounds) Then
```

```
            isBallRight = False
End If
```

Every Picture object has a boundary area, which we use to check collision with another boundary using bounds.IntersectsWith(). When we use this in an If statement, as above, we can check if any collision has occurred. Now test your code and see if the ball bounces off each wall.

Controlling the paddle

Now we have the ball bouncing, we need to create the paddle for the player to control, then assign it to the computer mouse for side-to-side movement. The paddle sprite is going to be another PictureBox control. Drag one from the toolbox onto the form, resize it to 100, 25 in the Size property and

BASIC ANALYSIS

```
pctPaddle.Left  = e.x - (pctPaddle.
width / 2)
```

The MouseMove subroutine comes with a variable called 'e' that you can use. All you need to do is map it to the horizontal x plane (left and right). Since we're using the left side of the paddle to match it to, we need to divide the width of the paddle by two, so that it matches to the centre of the paddle, not the far left.

TOP TIP
Most developers will refer to subroutines as 'subs'.

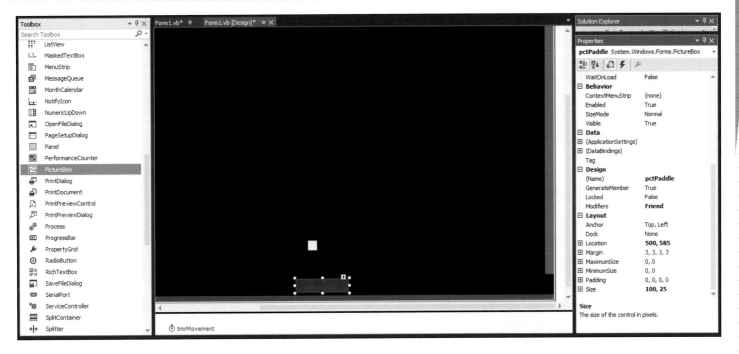

give it the name pctPaddle. Feel free to pick the colour by changing the BackColor value. Place the paddle at the bottom of the screen, just above pctWallBottom.

We now need to add the code that maps the mouse's horizontal movement (x) to the paddle. To get back to the Code view, click View on the top bar and select Code, or double-click the tmrMovement timer. There's a preset subroutine we can call for mouse movement events called MouseMove. To get to this, click on the dropdown box at the top of the Code view and select OblongOffensive Events, then in the dropdown box to the left of that select MouseMove. This will add all the necessary subroutines, start and end code. Add the following line of code with the MouseMove subroutine:

```
pctPaddle.Left = e.X - (pctPaddle.Width /
2)
```

Test the program and see if the mouse moves the pctPaddle left and right.

We now need to code the paddle so that the ball bounces off it when they collide together. To give the game an element of skill, we're also going to detect which side of the paddle has been hit and send the ball back in the opposite direction. For this, we're going to create our own subroutines, which are easy to code with the following syntax:

```
Private Sub NameofSub()

End Sub
```

▲ The paddle sprite is another PictureBox control.

Start with the keywords Private Sub, then give it a name of your choice. Always make it descriptive; the bracket after the name of your subroutine is an opportunity to pass data and variables into it if needed. To tell the complier we're finishing the subroutine, we use the keywords End Sub.

The subroutine we're going to create will check if the ball has touched the paddle and, depending on which half of the paddle it has touched, it will bounce off in the opposite direction. We're going to call the subroutine checkPaddleBounce. Add the following code underneath the End Sub of tmrMovement, but before End Class:

```
Private Sub checkPaddleBounce()

    Dim leftOffset As Integer
```

BASIC ANALYSIS

```
Private Sub checkBounce(ByVal collider
As PictureBox)
```

The big difference between this subroutine and the one for the paddle is that this subroutine has one of the PictureBox blocks pasted into it, which we rename 'collider'. We're being very efficient with our code here, as we could have created the code for each of the eight individual PictureBox blocks. Instead, we've created the collision code once and passed each block into it. This is why subroutines are awesome!

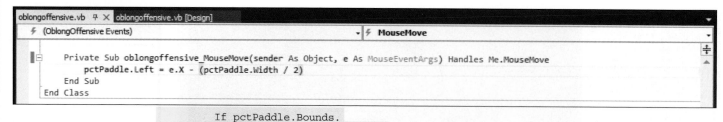

```
oblongoffensive.vb  ₽ X  oblongoffensive.vb [Design]
⚡ (OblongOffensive Events)                                    ⚡  MouseMove
    Private Sub oblongoffensive_MouseMove(sender As Object, e As MouseEventArgs) Handles Me.MouseMove
        pctPaddle.Left = e.X - (pctPaddle.Width / 2)
    End Sub
End Class
```

▲ Add the code that maps the mouse's horizontal movement (x) to the paddle.

```
        If pctPaddle.Bounds.
IntersectsWith(pctBall.Bounds) Then
            isBallUp = True

        leftOffset = pctPaddle.Left -
pctBall.Left

If leftOffset < -(pctPaddle.Width / 2)
Then
                isBallRight = True
            Else
                isBallRight = False
            End If
            ballSpeedHorizontal = (Rnd()
* 6) + 1
        End If
    End Sub
```

As we saw earlier, collision detection in Visual Basic uses the bounds.Intersectswith() function, which basically means the boundary of the shape touched another shape. So, pctPaddle.Bounds. IntersectsWith(pctBall.Bounds) is our conditional check if the paddle has touched the ball. If it has, we set isBallUp to true, which moves the ball back up.

To give the game increased user interaction, we need to check where on the paddle the ball has hit, so we can deflect it left or right. As there's no preset function in Visual Basic, to do this we're going to use a variable called leftOffset, which is the left value of the paddle minus the left value of the ball. We then use an If statement to check if that number is less than or greater than half the width of the paddle. We use our Boolean variable isBallRight to change the horizontal direction of the ball, by changing it to either true or false.

Our last piece of code for checkPaddleBounce() will be to randomise the speed of the deflection off the bat by giving our ballSpeedHorizontal variable a number between 1 and 7:

```
ballSpeedHorizontal = (Rnd() * 6) + 1
```

Now that we've created our subroutine, we'll need to call it from within the tmrMovement code by typing the name of it with brackets. Add the following code at the end of tmrMovement:

```
checkPaddleBounce()
```

Test your game now to see whether the paddle

> " Testing your game is very important to make sure everything works as intended "

deflects the ball left or right.

Making blocks

We need some blocks to hit in our arena, and we're going to use the PictureBox control from the toolbox to make each block. Create eight 50 x 50 PictureBoxes and colour each one. We don't have to rename the PictureBoxes, as Visual Basic will name them sequentially for us, and we'll refer to them only once in the code.

Just like the paddle, we're going to create a subroutine called checkBounce, to check if the block has been hit. Depending where the ball hits, we need to deflect the ball in the correct direction from all four sides. Create the following subroutine:

```
    Private Sub checkBounce(ByVal
collider As PictureBox)

        Dim topOffset As Integer
        Dim leftOffset As Integer

        If collider.Bounds.
IntersectsWith(pctBall.Bounds) Then

            topOffset = collider.Top -
pctBall.Top
            leftOffset = collider.Left -
pctBall.Left

            If topOffset > 0 And
topOffset
> leftOffset Then
                isBallUp = True
            ElseIf topOffset < 0 And
topOffset < leftOffset Then
                isBallUp = False
            End If
```

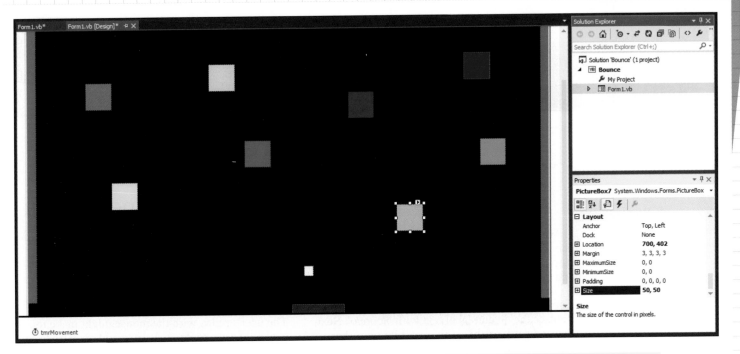

```
            If leftOffset < 0 And
leftOffset < topOffset Then
                isBallRight = True
            Else
                isBallRight = False
            End If
            collider.Left = -100
        End If
    End Sub
```

As we have to detect collision on the top, sides and bottom of each block, we're going to have two variables – leftOffset and topOffset – and use them in the same way as we did with the paddle, to check whether it needs to travel up or down, and left or right.

The only issue we have is that if the block has been hit, we need to make it disappear completely from the arena, so we set the x position of the PictureBox block (collider) to -100, which sends it far left out of the arena.

We now need to call our subroutine in tmrMovement next to where we called the checkPaddleBounce(), but this time we pass in each PictureBox. Add the following code to tmrMovement just above checkPaddleBounce():

```
checkBounce(PictureBox1)
        checkBounce(PictureBox2)
        checkBounce(PictureBox3)
        checkBounce(PictureBox4)
        checkBounce(PictureBox5)
        checkBounce(PictureBox6)
        checkBounce(PictureBox7)
```

▲ Use the PictureBox control to make each block.

TOP TIP
Testing your program is very important to make sure everything works as intended. Check to see what happens if you win the level or lose all of your lives before you let others play the game.

```
        checkBounce(PictureBox8)
```

Test your game to see if the blocks detect the ball, bounce in the correct direction and vanish when hit.

Creating a scoring system

To make this a proper game, we need a score that increases for every block hit and a set of lives, which will decrease every time the ball hits the bottom of the screen under the paddle. Also, we could give our game a cool title at the top, so players know the name of your amazing software!

We're going to need three label boxes from the toolbox, which will be our title, lives and score. Drag the first label onto the form from the toolbox and rename it lblLives, then change the text of the label to read 'Lives: 3'. Create a variable for our lives in our global variables section of the code (at the top) and give it the value of 3:

```
Dim lives As Integer = 3
```

To get the lives to count down, we need to add the following to the current If statement that checks if the ball has hit the bottom, in tmrMovement:

```
If pctBall.Bounds.
IntersectsWith(pctWallBottom.Bounds) Then
        isBallUp = True
        lives -= 1
        lblLives.Text = "Lives: " &
lives
```

Form1.vb*   Form1.vb [Design]*   ⊞ ✕

Bounce   _ ☐ ✕

Lives: 3   *Oblong Offensive*   Score: 0

▲ We need three label boxes from the toolbox for our title, lives and score.

```
            If lives = 0 Then
                tmrMovement.Enabled =
False
                MsgBox("Game Over")
                Me.Close()
            End If
```

We've had to put in another If statement to check when the lives equal 0. This then needs to stop the timer, display a 'Game Over' message box, and close the program.

To create a scoring system, we're going to use a new label from the toolbox and call it lblScore. Replace the default label text with 'Score:0'. Next, create a new variable at the top with our other global variables:

```
Dim score As Integer = 0
```

Add the following code to the checkBounce subroutine at the end, so that each block hit will increase the score variable by 10 and display the new score in lblScore.Text:

```
        collider.Left = -100
            score += 10
            lblScore.Text = "Score: " &
score
        End If
```

The last task with the score is to create an If statement that checks if the maximum score of 80 has been achieved, effectively clearing all blocks, stopping the timer, displaying a congratulations message, then quitting the program. Add the following code at the end of tmrMovement:

```
If score = 80 Then
            tmrMovement.Enabled = False
            MsgBox("Congratulations!  You
have cleared the level")
            Me.Close()
        End If
```

The last label box to add will just be the name of the game in the top-centre position. With all three boxes, feel free to change the fonts, background and size to match the style of your game.

Now test and play your game to see if everything works!

> ❝Give your game a cool title so players know the name of your amazing software!❞

Adding keyboard controls

The user's reflex with the mouse might make the game too easy, so if you want to add an extra layer of difficulty, we could change the control method of the paddle from the mouse to the keyboard. The first job is to disable the mouse control in the code, using the comment key (') in front of that line of code, so the complier ignores it:

```
Private Sub Form1_MouseMove(sender As
Object, e As MouseEventArgs) Handles
Me.MouseMove
        'pctPaddle.Left = e.X -
(pctPaddle.Width / 2)
    End Sub
```

If done correctly, the line should turn green, and we know that this line is temporarily removed from the game without having to delete what we've done. This also means we can switch back, should you want to re-enable the mouse, by taking out the comment symbol (') at the start of the line. This can be a useful trick when you're experimenting with an app or game.

We now need to code the paddle movement to use the keyboard. We do this using a method

EXPERIMENT

Depending on how difficult you want to make the game, you could try changing the numbers from 20 to a smaller value, which means it will take longer to move the paddle to the right position to deflect the ball. If you really want to throw the player, you could have different values for the left and right movement, so it takes time to adapt to the game!

```
 (OblongOffensive Events)                          ▼   MouseMove                                      ▼

     Private Sub checkPaddleBounce()                      ImeModeChanged

                                                          InputLanguageChanged
         'Dim topOffset As Integer
         Dim leftOffset As Integer                        InputLanguageChanging

                                                          Invalidated
         If pctPaddle.Bounds.IntersectsWith(p              KeyDown
             isBallUp = True
             leftOffset = pctPaddle.Left - pc              KeyPress
             If leftOffset < -(pctPaddle.Widtl             KeyUp
                 isBallRight = True
             Else                                          Layout
                 isBallRight = False                       Leave
             End If
             ballSpeedHorizontal = (Rnd() * 6              Load
         End If                                            LocationChanged
     End Sub
 End Sub                                                   LostFocus

                                                          MaximizedBoundsChanged
```

▲ Coding the paddle movement to use the keyboard.

"You can map almost any key from the keyboard to your controls"

very similar to the one we used for the mouse movement subroutine. Go into your code and select the Form events from the top dropdown menu, and this time select KeyDown from the right dropdown box.

This creates the subroutine code needed for Keyboard events. Add the following code to the subroutine, which will map the left and right arrow to the movement of the paddle:

```
If e.KeyValue = Keys.Left Then
        pctPaddle.Left -= 20
    End If


        If e.KeyValue = Keys.Right Then
            pctPaddle.Left += 20
        End If
```

With each If statement, we're binding the left and right arrow keys from the keyboard to increase the left-side position of the paddle by 20 or reduce the left-side position by 20. You can map almost any key from the keyboard to your

controls by changing Keys.Left to something like Keys.A. Alternatively, you can just type Keys. and Intellisense will give you a full list of keys to choose from.

If you want to move back to mouse control, you can comment out the code we've just entered – with the comment key (') on each line of both If statements – then uncomment the mouse control code. This method is really effective for testing parts of your code with new ideas, while not deleting anything you've previously coded.

Expanding the game
There are several ways you can expand the game to make it more challenging for the player:

- Change the speed of the ball (pctBall) for each block you've hit

- Shorten the width of the paddle (pctPaddle) every time your score increases

- Create more blocks of various sizes

- Change the form size and the position of the blocks

- Create 'power up' blocks that when collected could change the speed of the ball, alter the length of the paddle, increase the score or randomly choose one of the previous options.

- Randomise the Y coordinate position of the ball in form_load; this is code that runs when the form is loaded. You can access this by double-

```
⚡ (OblongOffensive Events)                                    ⚡ KeyDown
⊟    Private Sub OblongOffensive_KeyDown(sender As Object, e As KeyEventArgs) Handles Me.KeyDown
         If e.KeyValue = Keys.Left Then
             pctPaddle.Left -= 20
         End If

         If e.KeyValue = Keys.Right Then
             pctPaddle.Left += 20
         End If
     End Sub
```

▲ Map the left and right arrow to the movement of the paddle.

clicking the background of your form: pctBall.Top = (200 * Rnd()) + 30

● Randomise the Y coordinate position of the blocks in form_load: pctBall.Top = (200 * Rnd()) + 30

Final code

```
Public Class Form1

    Dim isBallRight As Boolean = False
    Dim isBallUp As Boolean = True
    Dim ballSpeedVertical As Integer = 3
    Dim ballSpeedHorizontal As Integer =
3

    Dim lives As Integer = 3
    Dim score As Integer = 0


    Private Sub tmrMovement_Tick(ByVal
sender As System.Object, ByVal e As
System.EventArgs) Handles tmrMovement.
Tick


        If isBallRight = True Then
pctBall.Left += ballSpeedHorizontal Else
pctBall.Left -= ballSpeedHorizontal
        If isBallUp = True Then pctBall.
Top -= ballSpeedVertical Else pctBall.Top
+= ballSpeedVertical


        If pctBall.Bounds.
IntersectsWith(pctWallBottom.Bounds) Then
            isBallUp = True
            lives -= 1
            lblLives.Text = "Lives: " &
lives
```

DID YOU KNOW?

The original 1976 Breakout was inspired by one of the very first arcade hits, Atari's 1972 game, Pong. Breakout was designed by Nolan Bushnell and Steve Bristow, but the code was written by Steve Wozniak with help from Steve Jobs, who would later go onto found Apple.

```
            If lives = 0 Then
                tmrMovement.Enabled =
False
                MsgBox("Game Over")
                Me.Close()
            End If
        ElseIf pctBall.Bounds.
IntersectsWith(pctWallTop.Bounds) Then
            isBallUp = False
        End If


        If pctBall.Bounds.
IntersectsWith(pctWallLeft.Bounds) Then
            isBallRight = True
        ElseIf pctBall.Bounds.
IntersectsWith(pctWallRight.Bounds) Then
            isBallRight = False
        End If


        checkBounce(PictureBox1)
        checkBounce(PictureBox2)
        checkBounce(PictureBox3)
        checkBounce(PictureBox4)
        checkBounce(PictureBox5)
        checkBounce(PictureBox6)
        checkBounce(PictureBox7)
        checkBounce(PictureBox8)


        checkPaddleBounce()


        If score = 80 Then
            tmrMovement.Enabled = False
            MsgBox("Congratulations! You
have cleared the level")
            Me.Close()
        End If

    End Sub


    Private Sub checkBounce(ByVal
collider As PictureBox)


        Dim topOffset As Integer
        Dim leftOffset As Integer


        If collider.Bounds.
IntersectsWith(pctBall.Bounds) Then
```

> **There are several ways you can expand the game to make it more challenging**

```
        topOffset = collider.Top -
pctBall.Top
        leftOffset = collider.Left -
pctBall.Left

        If topOffset > 0 And topOffset
> leftOffset Then
            isBallUp = True
        ElseIf topOffset < 0 And
topOffset < leftOffset Then
            isBallUp = False
        End If
        If leftOffset < 0 And
leftOffset < topOffset Then
            isBallRight = True
        Else
            isBallRight = False
        End If

        collider.Left = -100
        score += 10
        lblScore.Text = "Score: " &
score
      End If
    End Sub

    Private Sub checkPaddleBounce()

      Dim topOffset As Integer
      Dim leftOffset As Integer

      If pctPaddle.Bounds.
IntersectsWith(pctBall.Bounds) Then

          topOffset = pctPaddle.Top -
pctBall.Top
          leftOffset = pctPaddle.Left -
pctBall.Left

          If topOffset > 0 And topOffset
> leftOffset Then
              isBallUp = True
          ElseIf topOffset < 0 Then
              isBallUp = False
          End If
          If leftOffset < -(pctPaddle.
```

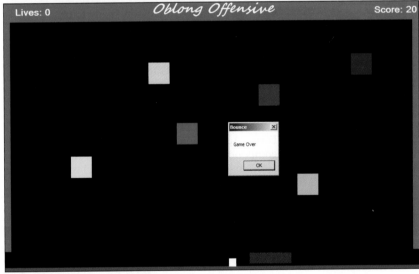

▲ Test and play your game to see if everything works!

```
Width / 2) And leftOffset < topOffset  Then
              isBallRight = True
          Else
              isBallRight = False
          End If
          ballSpeedHorizontal = (Rnd()
* 6) + 1
      End If

    End Sub

    Private Sub OblongOffensive_
MouseMove(sender As Object, e As
MouseEventArgs) Handles Me.MouseMove
        pctPaddle.Left = e.X -
(pctPaddle.Width / 2)
    End Sub
End Class
```

Build a Visual Basic app

Now you're getting to grips with Visual Basic, we can start to code more complex and exciting apps, such as this image viewer with built-in slideshow

Hopefully you're now ready to try something a little more complicated. To start with, we're going to create an image slideshow application that will use the PictureBox control, Timer control, and the Project Resource folder. This little app will import images from a computer and display them as a slideshow in a random order on a continuous loop.

Create a new project and select Windows Forms Application. Our form needs three basic components from the toolbox – PictureBox, Button and Timer. All of these controls can be found in the

Toolbox menu on the left-hand side of the screen. When you've selected one, you can draw the control on the form so you have full control over the size, layout and position of each component.

You can also change the name of the form by selecting it with a left mouse click, then choosing Text from the Properties window on the lower right-hand of the IDE. By default, it's named Form1: change it to something like frmPictureViewer. The only toolbox control we're going to rename is our button, which we can give the name btnStart, then change the button text to Start.

► Our form needs three basic components from the toolbox – PictureBox, Button and Timer.

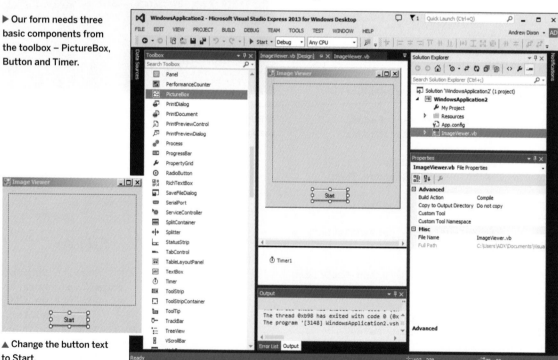

▲ Change the button text to Start.

DATA TYPES

Unlike SmallBASIC, VB needs to have a data type declared with the variable so the computer knows what type to expect, and can allocate the correct amount of memory. There are many different data types, but here are some of the most frequently used:

DATA TYPE	VALUE	EXAMPLE
Integer	Whole numbers	-32, 45, 1024
Single	Decimal numbers	3.145
String	Words (Text)	Kevin, Quirky
Boolean	True or False	True, False

▲ We need to add some images to our Resources folder, to be added into the random sequence.

You can drag the Timer icon on the form, but you won't see anything get added. Only the name Timer1 will appear underneath the form, with a Stopwatch icon, to show a timer has been added. The Timer control can repeat code at set time intervals, which will be useful when we want to display images for a certain amount of time. The interval value for the Timer control is measured in milliseconds, so every 1,000 ticks are equal to one second.

We also need to add images to our Resources folder, so that we have a bank of them ready to be added into the random sequence. Above the Properties window on the right of the screen, you'll see the Solution Explorer. This shows all of the forms you've created so far, and you should also find an option called My Project, which when double-clicked will give access to all of the options for the current application you're making. Find the Resources option, click 'Add resource' and

"My Project will give access to all of the options for the current app you're making"

finally select 'Existing resource'. This gives you a window to select the image files you'd like in your application. To keep things simple, just choose four images to import.

We're also going to declare a single variable for our application, as it will store a random number in memory that we can use to select which image will be displayed. All variables in Visual Basic start with Dim, then the name of the variable, and finally what data type. In this case, it will be an Integer (a whole number, without any decimal point):

```
Dim iCounter As Integer
```

Randomising a number is easy; you can call the Randomize() function to assign our variable a random number. The first number, 3, is the maximum we want to randomise, then we multiply that by Rnd(), which generates a random decimal number between 0 and 1. We add the +1 to the end, because if it generates 0 it will move to 1 instead:

```
Randomize()

iCounter = (3 * Rnd()) + 1
```

We then want to resize any given image to the width and height of our PictureBox control, so that all images appear with the same dimensions:

```
PictureBox1.SizeMode =
PictureBoxSizeMode.StretchImage
```

The timer now needs to be set, so it knows

BASIC ANALYSIS

```
PictureBox1.Image = My.Resources.ID_1001516
```

The line of code used to add images to the Picture window is simple: we first refer to the PictureBox by its name and property, picturebox1.image, then give it the location of the image file that we've uploaded to the Resources folder. In this example, our image was called ID_1001516. We never use the image file extension .jpg or .png; this would confuse Visual Basic, as most code uses a full stop to access further functions and properties.

how long to display each image until the next random picture. The interval number value is in milliseconds. Our timer has 3000, so it will display for three seconds:

```
Timer1.Interval = 3000
```

Everything is now ready, so we can add the code that will use our random number, and assign it to a particular picture with a basic If statement:

```
If iCounter = 1 Then
        PictureBox1.Image =
My.Resources.ID_1001516
    ElseIf iCounter = 2 Then
        PictureBox1.Image =
My.Resources.ID_100221425
    ElseIf iCounter = 3 Then
        PictureBox1.Image =
My.Resources.ID_10022176
    Else
        PictureBox1.Image =
My.Resources.ID_10029497
End If
```

This is all the code we'll need inside the Timer1 control. Our final step will be to add code to the Start button (btnStart), which will activate the timer. Double-click the Start button and add the following code inside it. This will set the Timer Interval to a quicker value; otherwise, we'd have to wait three seconds for the first image to appear. To activate the timer and effectively start the program, we set the Enabled property to true:

```
Timer1.Interval = 10

Timer1.Enabled = True
```

Run the program with the Start play button on the top bar, or press F5, when you have all the code in the correct place:

```
Public Class Form1

    Private Sub Timer1_Tick(sender As
Object, e As EventArgs) Handles Timer1.
```

EXPERIMENT

Try adding more pictures to the Resource folder, then change the code to accommodate the new images. For each new image, you'll have to increase the random number generated, currently (3 * Rnd()) + 1, then add to the PictureBox If statement using Elseif. The last image added will just be Else not Elseif.

CODING KEYWORDS

GUI: Graphical User Interface. The layout, size and appearance of your application, and all the buttons, icons, menus and sliders you use to control it.

```
Tick

        Dim iCounter As Integer
        Randomize()
        iCounter = (3 * Rnd()) + 1
        PictureBox1.SizeMode =
PictureBoxSizeMode.StretchImage
        Timer1.Interval = 3000

        If iCounter = 1 Then
            PictureBox1.Image =
My.Resources.ID_1001516
        ElseIf iCounter = 2 Then
            PictureBox1.Image =
My.Resources.ID_100221425
        ElseIf iCounter = 3 Then
            PictureBox1.Image =
My.Resources.ID_10022176
        Else
            PictureBox1.Image =
My.Resources.ID_10029497
        End If
    End Sub

    Private Sub BtnStart_Click(sender As
Object, e As EventArgs) Handles BtnStart.
Click
        Timer1.Interval = 10
```

▲ Our program randomly displays one of four images.

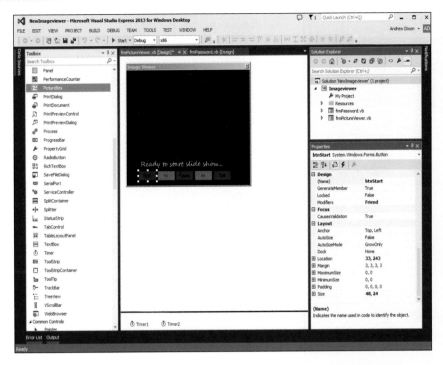

```
        Timer1.Enabled = True
    End Sub
End Class
```

▲ Add some style and
functionality to your app.

Our finished program will now display one of
the four images in a random order every three
seconds. We can change the speed of the rotation
by altering the value of Timer1.Interval; the higher
the number, the longer it will stay on each image
before moving to the next.

Just remember that our pictures used filenames
like ID_1001516. Yours will be different, so make
sure you use the same names when you're coding
the PictureBox1.image section as the names inside
your Resources folder. Intellisense is useful here,
and can help you get the job done faster.

Changing styles

We now have a good working prototype, but we
can give it some style and functionality. Let's first
work on the GUI of our application.

Visual Basic always defaults to a drab grey
colour, so to change our background we need to
select the form with a left mouse click and find
BackColor from the Properties menu (on the

EXPERIMENT

If you want to change the speed of the fade-in effect,
try changing the value in Me.Opacity += 0.01 to more
decimal places e.g. 0.001.

"Change the speed of the rotation by altering the value of the Timer1.Interval"

bottom right) and change this to black. Next, we're
going to change the window appearance to give it a
sleeker look with no icon or minimise buttons. Find
FormBorderStyle in the Properties menu and select
FixedToolWindowi. This means we can move the
image viewer around the screen, but the user can't
resize the window with the mouse.

Our Start button now looks out of place, with
the cool new look we're giving our image viewer
program, so let's change its appearance. Make the
following changes from the Properties window:
change FlatStyle to 'popup', and BackColor to a
dark grey. To change the font colour of the button,
you need to choose a colour from ForeColor.

The last change to our form is a caption
underneath each picture. To do this, we'll need
a label box from the toolbox. Position this
underneath the photo, and change the colour and
font to suit your theme. By default, we can add the
phrase "Ready to start slide show..." by editing the
Text property of the label. To set the caption when
each image is loaded, we're going to edit the If
statement in Timer1 with the highlighted code, but
the message can be changed to suit your images:

```
If iCounter = 1 Then
            PictureBox1.Image =
My.Resources.ID_1001516
            Caption.Text = "A beautiful
image"
        ElseIf iCounter = 2 Then
PictureBox1.Image = My.Resources.
ID_100221425
            Caption.Text = " I love the
colours here "
        ElseIf iCounter = 3 Then
            PictureBox1.Image =
My.Resources.ID_10022176
            Caption.Text = "I wish I was
back there now!"
        Else
PictureBox1.Image = My.Resources.
ID_10029497
            Caption.Text = "Simply
stunning"
        End If
```

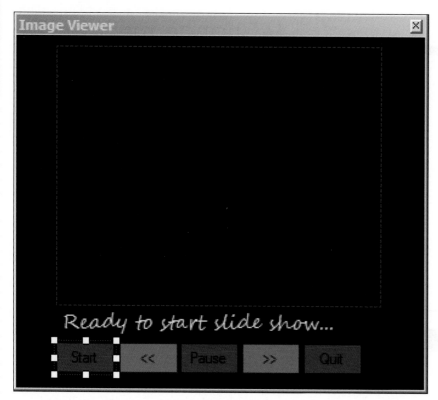

Image Viewer

Ready to start slide show...

Start   <<   Pause   >>   Quit

▲ Our toolbar's buttons can manually change the speed of the image transitions.

Visual Basic doesn't give us much in the way of applying effects to our pictures, but we do have an Opacity property with our form that can give a fade-in effect. To use this, we need to add another Timer control and use a Do While loop to check the opacity value, before gradually increasing it until it gets to 1, which is fully visible. Add a new timer (Timer2) from the toolbox and add the following code:

```
Timer2.Interval = 30
    Do While Me.Opacity < 1
       Me.Opacity += 0.01
    Loop
```

Every time we load a new random picture, we'll need to reset the opacity down to a nearly invisible value, then our Do While loop in Timer2 will kick in and slowly return the value back to completely visible (1). Add the following code to the Timer1 PictureBox If statement:

```
        If iCounter = 1 Then
Me.Opacity = 0.001
            PictureBox1.Image =
My.Resources.ID_1001516
Caption.Text = "A beautiful image"
        ElseIf iCounter = 2 Then
Me.Opacity = 0.001
            PictureBox1.Image =
```

```
My.Resources.ID_100221425
Caption.Text = "I love the colours here"
        ElseIf iCounter = 3 Then
Me.Opacity = 0.001
            PictureBox1.Image =
My.Resources.ID_10022176
Caption.Text = "Wish I was back there
now!"
        Else
            Me.Opacity = 0.001
            PictureBox1.Image =
My.Resources.ID_10029497
Caption.Text = "Simply stunning"
        End If
    End Sub
```

We'll also need to edit our Start button (btnStart), so that we now start to enable both timers. Add the following to the existing code:

```
Timer2.Enabled = True
```

Making a toolbar
For our next change, we're going to create a custom toolbar with buttons that can manually change the speed of the image transitions to be faster or slower than our default value. We'll also add Pause and Quit buttons. All of our buttons will have the same style as our Start button, but we can alternate our grey colours to make things more interesting.

Our Pause button will effectively stop both timers, so any picture currently onscreen will stay there until the Start button is pressed again. Add the following code by double-clicking on the Pause button on the form:

```
Timer1.Enabled = False
```

```
Timer2.Enabled = False
```

The Quit button will close our app. Double-click the Quit button and add the following line of code:

```
Close()
```

The Speedup button (>>) will shorten the Timer1.interval value by 500 milliseconds (half a second), but as we've mentioned before we can't go below 0 or we'll get a critical error and our app will crash. To prevent this, we're going to put an If statement to check if the interval value has dropped below 1000 and, if it has, we'll hide the button, so the user can't click it anymore. Double-click the Slowdown button (<<) and add the following code:

```
Timer1.Interval = Timer1.Interval - 500
```

"Our Slowdown button will increase the interval value of the Timer1 by 500 "

||||||||||||||||||||||||||||||||||||||||||||||||||||||||||

```
If Timer1.Interval < 1000 Then
    btnSpeedUp.Visible = False
End If
```

Our Slowdown button will increase the interval value of the Timer1 by 500 milliseconds. We'll also need a short If statement that brings back the visibility of the Speedup button if it's been hidden by the other speed control button. Double-click the Slowdown button and add this code:

```
Timer1.Interval = Timer1.Interval + 500
    If Timer1.Interval > 1000 Then
        btnSpeedUp.Visible = True
    End If
```

Final code

```
Public Class frmPictureViewer

    Private Sub Button1_Click(ByVal
sender As System.Object, ByVal e As
System.EventArgs) Handles btnStart.Click
        Timer1.Interval = 3000
        Timer1.Enabled = True
        Timer2.Enabled = True
        Caption.Text = "Getting ready to
start...."
    End Sub


    Private Sub Timer1_Tick(ByVal sender
As System.Object, ByVal e As System.
EventArgs) Handles Timer1.Tick
        Dim iCounter As Integer
        Randomize()
        iCounter = (4 * Rnd()) + 1
        PictureBox1.SizeMode =
PictureBoxSizeMode.StretchImage


        If iCounter = 1 Then
Me.Opacity = 0.001
            PictureBox1.Image =
My.Resources.ID_1001516
Caption.Text = "A beautiful image"
```

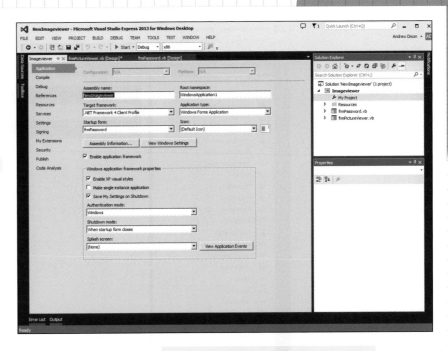

▲ Under the Application menu, you'll find a Startup form option, where you can select any form you've made so far.

```
        ElseIf iCounter = 2 Then
Me.Opacity = 0.001
            PictureBox1.Image =
My.Resources.ID_100221425
Caption.Text = "I love the colours here"
        ElseIf iCounter = 3 Then
Me.Opacity = 0.001
            PictureBox1.Image =
My.Resources.ID_10022176
Caption.Text = "Wish I was back there
now!"
        Else
            Me.Opacity = 0.001
            PictureBox1.Image =
My.Resources.ID_10029497
Caption.Text = "Simply stunning"
        End If
    End Sub

    End Sub


    Private Sub Timer2_Tick(ByVal sender
As System.Object, ByVal e As System.
EventArgs) Handles Timer2.Tick
        Timer2.Interval = 30
        Do While Me.Opacity < 1
            Me.Opacity += 0.01
        Loop
    End Sub


    Private Sub btnQuit_Click(ByVal
sender As System.Object, ByVal e As
System.EventArgs) Handles btnQuit.Click
        Close()
    End Sub
```

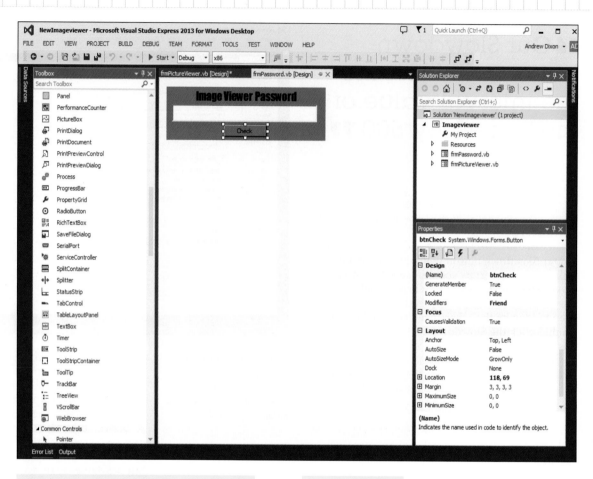

▶ To complete our image viewer, we've added a password screen.

```
      Private Sub btnPause_Click(ByVal
sender As System.Object, ByVal e As
System.EventArgs) Handles btnPause.Click
          Timer1.Enabled = False
          Timer2.Enabled = False
      End Sub


      Private Sub btnSlowDown_Click(ByVal
sender As System.Object, ByVal e As
System.EventArgs) Handles btnSlowDown.
Click
          Timer1.Interval = Timer1.Interval
+ 500
          If Timer1.Interval > 1000 Then
              btnSpeedUp.Visible = True
          End If
      End Sub


      Private Sub btnSpeedUp_Click(ByVal
sender As System.Object, ByVal e As
System.EventArgs) Handles btnSpeedUp.
Click
          Timer1.Interval = Timer1.Interval
- 500

          If Timer1.Interval < 1000 Then
              btnSpeedUp.Visible = False
```

```
          End If
      End Sub


  End Class
```

Adding security

To complete our image viewer, we're going to add a security feature that will stop any unwanted users from accessing our slideshow. We'll need to add another form, which you can access under the Project menu, selecting Add Windows Form. We'll call this form frmPassword.

On our password form, we're going to add a label for a title, which can say Image Viewer Password, by changing the Text property. We'll also need a textbox, call it txtPassword, so the user can type in the password and a button (btnCheck) to check if the password is correct. You can apply all the style changes we've done for frmImageViewer, such as colour, fonts and form style, to give it the feel that it all belongs in one application.

We'll set the password in the code using an If statement. If the user enters the correct password, we're going to hide the visibility of our password form, then enable the visibility of our frmPictureViewer. If the user enters anything but

"Why not make your own logo that represents you or your software studio?"

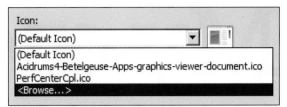

▲ Give your application or game its own icon for a more professional finish.

the password, we'll use a neat pop-up box function called MsgBox that can display a message in a pop-up screen with a single OK button, to cancel the message and return back to the password screen.

When you've created and edited the button, double-click it and add the following code:

```
If txtPassword.Text = "letmein" Then
         Me.Visible = False
         frmPictureViewer.Visible =
True
    Else
         MsgBox("Unauthorised!")
    End If
```

In this example, we've used the password 'letmein', but feel free to change it to something more personal and certainly more secure!

It's no good having a password box if anyone can see what you're typing onscreen, so we're going to stealth our text behind a symbol. Simply select our textbox and find the property value PasswordChar on the right-hand side of the screen. Enter an asterix symbol (*) in the field, and this will instruct the computer to display that symbol whenever the user types on the keyboard.

As we've made this form last, the program won't be the first form we see, as Visual Basic will always default to the first form created – in this case, the form with our slideshow. To change the order, we need to go back to My Project in the Solutions Window. Under the Application menu, you'll find a Startup form option, where you can select any form you've made so far. Change this to frmPassword.

Now test your program by clicking Run on the toolbar or pressing F5.

Making your app ready to run
We have a good working program, but don't really want to load Visual Studio, then run the program each time we want to see our slideshow. Whenever you run your code, Visual Studio compiles it in a single executable file (EXE). Basically, it takes the Basic code we write and

TOP TIP
If you want, you can rename the EXE file with a right-click, then select Rename.

converts it into a series of instructions that your PC or laptop can understand.

To find the executable file, go to the Project file on your computer, and you'll see a folder called Bin. Inside, there's another folder called Debug. This will contain the single EXE file of your complied code. You can drag this out of the folder and onto your Windows desktop.

To run an EXE file, just double-click on it. Your program will then appear and work its magic. The great thing is that you now have a version of your game or app that other people can run, whether they have Visual Basic installed or not. This is a great way of distributing your app or game.

Changing an icon file
The icon for your executable file will be the default Windows icon, but we can change that to an exciting graphic that better represents your application by using the Project Settings window, where we changed the load order of the forms. Next to this, there's a dropdown box under the heading Icon, where we can browse for a new image or select one we've already used.

Icon files aren't like normal image files such as GIF, JPEG or PNG. They have their own file type, ICO, which indicates they're icons used on files. You either need to download some free ICO files for your application from the internet, or you can convert an image you've already made using an image editor that supports exporting to the ICO format. If you need something to do the job, we'd recommend the popular free image editor, IrfanView. You can get this from www.irfanview.com. Click on browse and find a new icon image.

When you've changed the icon for the application, run the program again with F5 or the Run button. Check the Debug folder, and the new EXE file will be there, with your new icon image ready for you to use or distribute to others.

Giving your application or game its own icon won't change the way it works, but it will add a more professional finish to the final product. You could even make your own logo that represents you or your software studio, which you can use within all of your programs. It will give them some identify and tell the world who's made this awesome software! ●

My awesome game

It's time to put our Visual Basic skills to the test with one final, spectacular game. Prepare to find out for yourself why Gravity Sucks!

For our final program, we're going to create another addictive game called Gravity Sucks. This will feature a menu screen, where the user can start a new game, quit the program and display the current high score. This game will test the user's skill and reactions by jumping the player block through random gaps while it's constantly pulled down by gravity. If the block touches the scenery, the game ends and the user's score, which constantly counts up, is displayed.

The building blocks

Create a new project and, again, choose Windows Forms Application. First, we're going to create the game environment with the following features. Set the current form name to MainGame with a width of 763 and a height of 537 using the Size property. Change the FormBorderStyle to none, so we don't see the top bar on the form. Finally, you can default the game to the centre of the screen by changing StartPosition to CenterScreen. Set the background

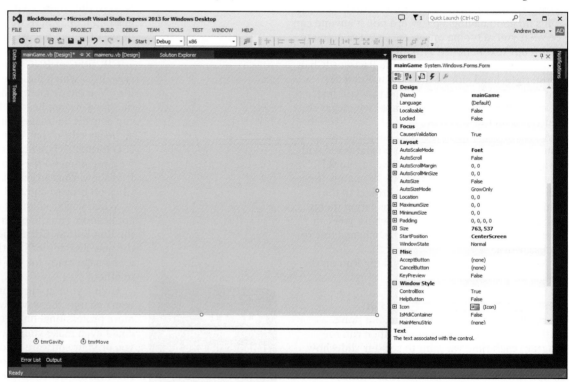

▲ Set the current form name to MainGame with a width of 763 and a height of 537 using the Size property.

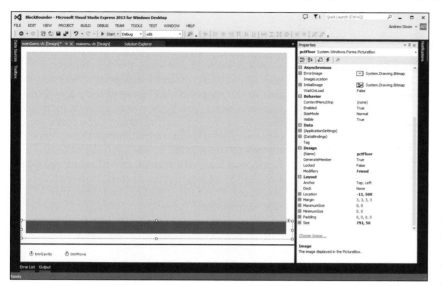

> **❝ If the block touches the scenery, the game ends and the user's score is displayed ❞**

▲ Insert a PictureBox on the page and call it pctFloor. Set the location to -11, 500.

colour of the game using the BackColor property.

Next, insert a PictureBox on the page and call it pctFloor, then manually set the Size property, width and height to 751, 50. Set the location to -11, 500 using the Location property. Change the colour to anything you want.

Now, insert another PictureBox on the page, and call it pctCeiling, then manually set the Size property, width and height to 791, 50. Set the location to -11, -26 using the Location property. Again, change the colour to anything you want.

Then, insert another PictureBox on the page, and call it pctBottom1, then manually set the Size property, width and height to 82, 339. Set the location to 82, 339 using the Location property. Change the colour to anything you want.

Next, insert another PictureBox and call it pctBottom2, then manually set the Size property, width and height to 82, 339. Set the location to 671,

347 using the Location property. Change the colour to anything you want.

Insert another PictureBox and call it pctTop1, then manually set the Size property, width and height to 82, 339. Set the location to 305, -208 using the Location property. Change the colour to anything you want.

Insert another PictureBox and call it pctTop2, then manually set the Size property, width and height to 82, 339. Set the location to 671, -208 using the Location property. Change the colour to anything you want.

Finally, insert a PictureBox on the page, and call it pctBounder, then manually set the Size property, width and height to 60, 60. Set the location to 118, 177 using the Location property. This will be our game character, so give them a cool colour, different from all the other PictureBoxes.

The core working code

We now have all the graphics we need for our main game. Next, we need to add two timers: one will move the scenery, the other will control gravity. We also need a label box to show the score counting up:

● Create a new label box called lblScore and set its location to 12, 508. Feel free to change the background colour of the label to match pctFloor, then change the height and colour of the font so it stands out

● Insert a Timer and call it tmrGravity

● Insert another Timer and call it tmrMove

Let's start adding the code to make this game work. We're going to need to set some global variables that all of our subroutines can access,

▼ Insert another PictureBox on the page, and call it pctCeiling, then set the Size property, width and height to 791, 50.

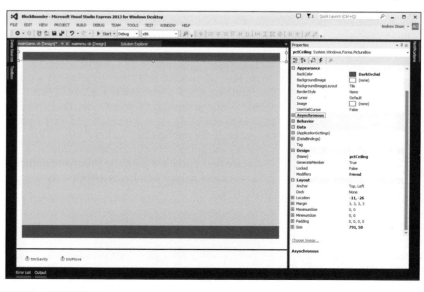

►

CODING KEYWORDS

Class: Large applications and games need to be written in sections. In Visual Basic, these chunks of code are called classes.

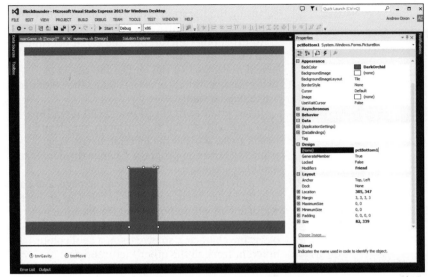

▲ Insert a PictureBox and call it pctBottom1. Set the Size property, width and height to 82, 339.

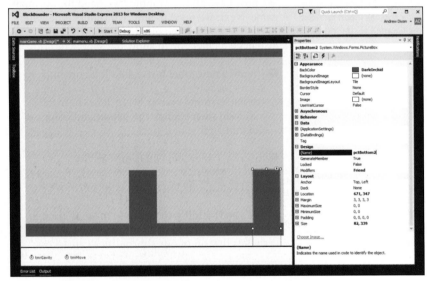

▲ Insert a PictureBox and call it pctBottom2. Set the location to 671, 347 .

such as score, game speed and gravity strength. To do this, we need to add them to an area called Declarations. Click View on the top bar of the Visual Studio screen and select Code. This will take us to our Code view, which should only have the name of the public class and end class. Our variables are going between these two values.

Create four variables with the following names, data types and values within the public class maingame:

```
Dim GravitySpeed As Integer = 0
```

```
Dim RandomNumber As Integer
```

```
Dim GameSpeed As Integer = 4
```

```
Dim PlayerScore As Integer = 0
```

While we're in this view, we can code the movement of our player block pctBounder and map that to the spacebar. At the top of the page, above the class name, you'll see two dropdown menus: the one on the left has the name of the form, the other will say Declarations. Change the one on the left to (maingame events) and the other to KeyDown. This will give us the subroutine code needed for addressing user interaction with the keyboard. Enter the following code into this new subroutine:

```
If e.KeyValue = Keys.Space Then
    tmrMove.Enabled = True
    tmrGavity.Enabled = True
    GravitySpeed = -14
End If
```

This code will run every time the user presses the spacebar. By starting both timers from the spacebar, it means the game won't start automatically and everything can begin on the first spacebar press. By setting the GravitySpeed to a negative number, it will have the effect of moving the player block towards the top of the screen.

Go back to the design screen of the game and double-click the gravity timer (tmrGravity), so that Visual Studio can add the automatic subroutine code for you. In that subroutine, add the following code:

```
pctBounder.Top += GravitySpeed
```

```
GravitySpeed += 1
```

```
PlayerScore += 1
```

```
lblScore.Text = PlayerScore
```

This code sets our player block to move by -14, sending our block upwards, then we bring it back down with the next line GravitySpeed += 1. tmrGravity is also the timer that we're going to

BASIC ANALYSIS

```
MsgBox("Your score: " & PlayerScore)
```

Our last MsgBox was the one we used on the password screen for the image viewer app. That one just displayed text, using the text inside the quotation marks. However, using the ampersand symbol (&), we can insert a variable into the sentence.

"This first block of code sets our PicureBoxes to move left gradually "

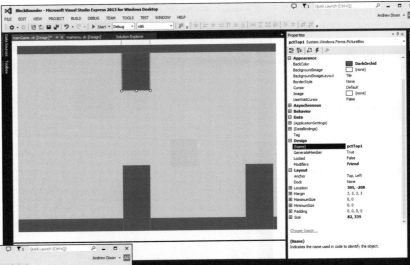

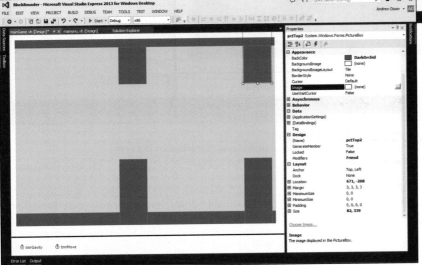

▲ Insert another PictureBox and call it pctTop1. Set the location to 305, -208.

```
pctTop2.Left -= GameSpeed
```

This first block of code sets our PictureBoxes to move left gradually by the variable GameSpeed, which we initially set to 4 in our global declarations.

```
If pctTop1.Left < -pctTop1.Width Then
        RandomNumber = -((Rnd() *
250) + 40)
        pctTop1.Top = RandomNumber
        pctBottom1.Top = pctTop1.Top
+ 555
        pctTop1.Left = Me.Width
        pctBottom1.Left = Me.Width
    End If
```

```
    If pctTop2.Left < -pctTop2.Width
Then
        RandomNumber = -((Rnd() *
250) + 40)
        pctTop2.Top = RandomNumber
        pctBottom2.Top = pctTop2.Top
+ 555
        pctTop2.Left = Me.Width
        pctBottom2.Left = Me.Width
    End If
```

This next block randomises the position of both sets of top/bottom PictureBoxes, while still maintaining the same gap length. After the first two obstacles have passed, the code will start changing the dimensions of the PictureBoxes. If you've followed the dimensions and locations of the PictureBoxes printed at the start of the project, all of the numbers inside this block will maintain the same gap width.

use to count our score: by getting PlayerScore to increase by 1 every time, the counter ticks, then we display that number by setting lblScore.text to equal the variable PlayerScore.

The last piece of code we need to get the game working is the code for the other timer (tmrMove). This timer will move our blocks across the screen, randomise the location of the gap to jump through and detect any collision between our player block and the rest of the scenery. Double-click the tmrMove icon at the bottom of your form, which, again, will take you into Code view and automatically add the required subroutine code. Enter the following in the subroutine:

```
pctBottom1.Left -= GameSpeed
```

```
pctBottom2.Left -= GameSpeed
```

```
pctTop1.Left -= GameSpeed
```

▲ Insert PictureBox and call it pctTop2, then set the Size property, width and height to 82, 339.

▶ Insert a PictureBox and call it pctBounder, then set the Size property, width and height to 60, 60.

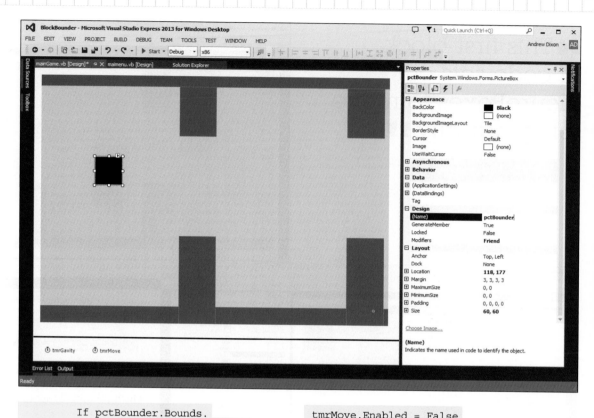

```
        If pctBounder.Bounds.
IntersectsWith(pctBottom1.Bounds) _
        Or pctBounder.Bounds.
IntersectsWith(pctBottom2.Bounds) _
        Or pctBounder.Bounds.
IntersectsWith(pctTop1.Bounds) _
        Or pctBounder.Bounds.
IntersectsWith(pctTop2.Bounds) _
        Or pctBounder.Bounds.
IntersectsWith(pctFloor.Bounds) _
        Or pctBounder.Bounds.
IntersectsWith(pctCeiling.Bounds) Then

tmrGavity.Enabled = False
```

```
tmrMove.Enabled = False
MsgBox("Your score: " & PlayerScore)
```

The final code block in tmrMove will deal with collision detection of our player pctBounder against the boundaries of all other PicturesBoxes on the screen. If collision is detected, both timers will be turned off, effectively halting the game, and a message box will appear with the PlayerScore variable, which stopped counting when the timers were disabled. As the If statement has six conditions, we can use space underscore space (_) at the end of each one, which allows us to use the line underneath, and the computer will still treat them as if they're on one line. We're now in a position where we can test our game and solve any errors. Run the program and try your new game!

Making menus

At the moment, our game doesn't end very well, as we have to manually stop the code from working. It would also be nice to introduce our game and display the highest score made in one session. What can we do? We can make a menu screen that will appear at the start and end of the game.

Create a new form called mainmenu. The size and style of this form are down to you; just make sure that it feels like it belongs to the rest of the application. Use colours that match the main game, and add the following controls from the toolbox:

▼ Try changing the GravitySpeed variable in the KeyDown subroutine from -14 to a higher or smaller value.

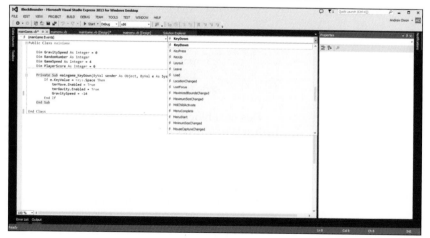

- Create a new button called btnStart and change the button text to New Game. Both are in the Properties window. Make any cosmetic changes you feel would match your game.

- Create a new button called btnQuit and change the button text to Quit Game – both are in the Properties menu.

- Create a new label called lblHighScore and change the label text to 0. This box will display the best score in one session, so make it big and give it a colour that stands out.

- Try adding new features to the GUI, such as a label for the game's name and one that will say High Score, which can be placed next to lblHighScore.

Double-click btnStart and add the following code:

```
mainGame.Visible = True
```

```
Me.Visible = False
```

These simply hide the menu screen and will show the game screen. Don't forget, you can't refer to form mainmenu by name, as we're currently working on the form, so we'll use Me.Visible to refer to our menu screen form.

Go back to the design screen and double-click the btnQuit button, then add the following code that will quit the game completely:

```
Close()
```

We'll also have to go back to the maingame and change the end of our game, so that we go back to the menu and take the high score with us. Go back into tmrMove and add the following code underneath our MsgBox code:

```
If frmMenu.lblHighScore.Text <
PlayerScore Then
    frmMenu.lblHighScore.Text =
PlayerScore
End If
```

```
Me.Close()
frmMenu.Visible = True
```

The first If statement checks whether the text in the highscore label on the mainmenu form is less than the PlayerScore variable. If it is, the new high score goes to the lblHighScore label; if it's not, the existing value stays. This means that only the highest score will appear on the menu screen.

TAKE IT FURTHER

You don't have to stop developing now. Why not try some other ideas to take this game further?

- Try to add images into the PictureBoxes: for example, the player sprite could have a face instead of being a 60 x 60 black block. Create a 60 x 60 image and load that into the pctBounder box. You could use similar graphics for the floor, ceiling and blocks to give the game a more professional look.

- Change the menu screen so that the player can start either an easy game or a hard game by changing the values of GravitySpeed.

- To increase the game's difficulty, you could make the width of the screen shorter as the game progresses.

- Each game could start with a random gravity value between two numbers. Just make sure that the number isn't too low or too high.

- Add powerup PictureBoxes on the screen, which, when collected (touched then made invisible), can change the speed of the game or give a +500 boost to the player's score.

- Change the gap between the top and bottom PictureBoxes so that the player has a smaller gap to jump through.

- Create a large GAME OVER label and hide it until the player gets their score.

> ## 66 To increase the game's difficulty, you could make the width of the screen shorter 99

The last two lines of code close the maingame form and make the main menu visible again. If we were to use the line Me.Visible = True, then when we start a new game we'll start at the end of the previous game. The Me.Close() code will force a new game to start from the beginning.

Test the game to make sure all the new features on the menu screen work correctly, with run or F5.

Tweaking the variables

Hopefully, we now have a working game that we can tweak to make it suitable for other users. Because we have used variables for our game engine, we can change their values to alter the behaviour of the player sprite, or the gravity. Experiment with the following variables in your code to see how each change affects the gameplay:

- Change the GravitySpeed variable in the KeyDown subroutine from -14 to a higher or smaller value. What effect does that have on our player sprite pctBounder?

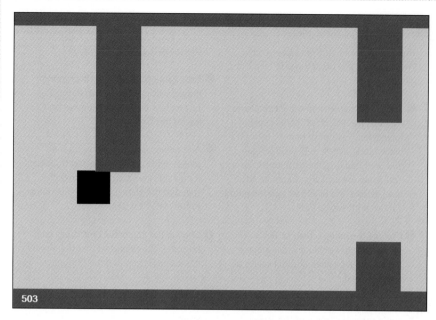

503

▲ If collision is detected, both timers will be turned off, effectively halting the game,

▲ Our game now displays the highest score made in one session.

▶ Use MenuStrip to add options to the top of the menu screen,

● Change the GameSpeed variable value in the Declarations top section from 4 to a higher or lower value. How does that affect the difficulty of the game?

● Change the PlayerScore value in tmrGravity from 1 to a higher number. How does that affect the score in the game?

Extending the game

You might also want to expand the game to make it progressively more difficult the longer the player survives. Enter the code at the start of the tmrMove subroutine:

```
If (PlayerScore > 400) And (PlayerScore <
1000) Then
        GameSpeed = 6
    ElseIf PlayerScore > 1000 Then
        GameSpeed = 8
End If
```

● Change the GravitySpeed variable in the tmrGravity subroutine from 1 to a higher value. What effect does that have on our player sprite pctBounder?

The If statement above has a more complex condition to check, just like the collision detection If statement in tmrMove. If you want two conditions that need to be met, we'd put each condition criteria into brackets separated by the

Gravity Sucks: Main Menu

Gravity Sucks

New Game

Quit Game

High Score: 0

▲ Here's our finished game!

❝ You might want to expand the game to make it progressively more difficult ❞

And operator. In the code that we've just entered, we're checking if the PlayerScore variable is between 401 and 999: if it is, it increases the game speed up by two. Then, if the player gets over 999, the speed again raises by another two. As the player progress through the game, the speed of the obstacles increases to raise the difficulty.

Finishing touches
To give our new game some finishing touches, we're going to add options to the top of the menu screen, very similar to most software programs, where you have File, Edit and About at the top of the window. Open the toolbox and find

MenuStrip, and drag this to your mainmenu form.

You now have a menu bar across the top with no options inside, so click on the menustrip and add our first option, File. You'll notice that you get branch-out options underneath our new File menu, so let's add Quit. Double-click on Quit when you've made it, and you'll get the Code view for that option, and enter the code:

```
Close()
```

Go back to the form design and add another option next to File called Help. Underneath this, add a new option called About. This is going to bring up a message box telling the user about you as a developer, or your software house credits. Enter the following code, but change the content of the message box:

```
MSGbox("Gravity Sucks - Coded by ADX")
```

Final code

```
Public Class mainGame

    Dim GravitySpeed As Integer = 0
    Dim RandomNumber As Integer
    Dim GameSpeed As Integer = 4
    Dim PlayerScore As Integer = 0

    Private Sub maingame_KeyDown(ByVal
sender As Object, ByVal e As System.
Windows.Forms.KeyEventArgs) Handles
Me.KeyDown
        If e.KeyValue = Keys.Space Then
            tmrMove.Enabled = True
            tmrGavity.Enabled = True
            GravitySpeed = -14 'Height of
the block jump
        End If
    End Sub

    Private Sub tmrGavity_Tick(ByVal
sender As System.Object, ByVal e As
System.EventArgs) Handles tmrGavity.Tick
        pctBounder.Top += GravitySpeed
        GravitySpeed += 1 'strength of
gravity
        PlayerScore += 1
        lblScore.Text = PlayerScore
    End Sub

    Private Sub tmrMove_Tick(ByVal sender
As System.Object, ByVal e As System.
EventArgs) Handles tmrMove.Tick

        If (PlayerScore > 400) And
(PlayerScore < 1000) Then
```

Teach Your Kids to Code

► Add Quit underneath your new File menu.

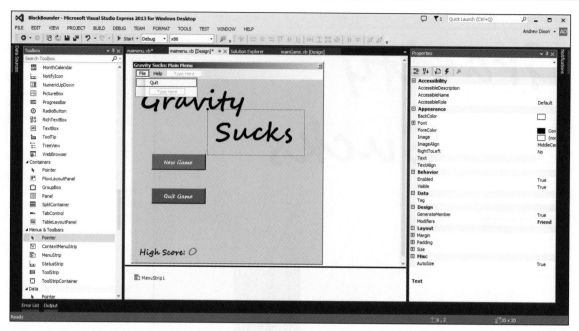

▼ Underneath Help, add a new option called About.

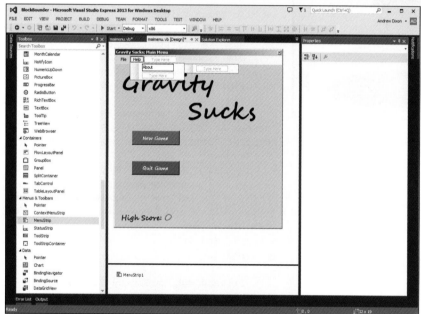

"Change the parameters of the If statement to suit your game"

```
        RandomNumber = -((Rnd() *
250) + 40)
        pctTop1.Top = RandomNumber
        pctBottom1.Top = pctTop1.Top
+ 555
        pctTop1.Left = Me.Width
        pctBottom1.Left = Me.Width
    End If

    If pctTop2.Left < -pctTop2.Width
Then
        RandomNumber = -((Rnd() *
250) + 40)
        pctTop2.Top = RandomNumber
        pctBottom2.Top = pctTop2.Top
+ 555
        pctTop2.Left = Me.Width
        pctBottom2.Left = Me.Width
    End If

    If pctBounder.Bounds.
IntersectsWith(pctBottom1.Bounds) _
        Or pctBounder.Bounds.
```

```
        GameSpeed = 6
    ElseIf PlayerScore > 1000 Then
        GameSpeed = 8
    End If

    pctBottom1.Left -= GameSpeed
    pctBottom2.Left -= GameSpeed
    pctTop1.Left -= GameSpeed
    pctTop2.Left -= GameSpeed

    If pctTop1.Left < -pctTop1.Width
Then
```

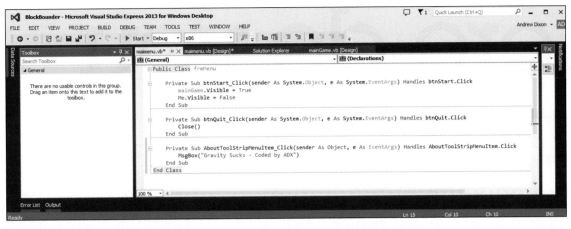

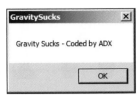

▲ Tell the user about you as a developer.

◀ Make sure you change the content of the message box (in red).

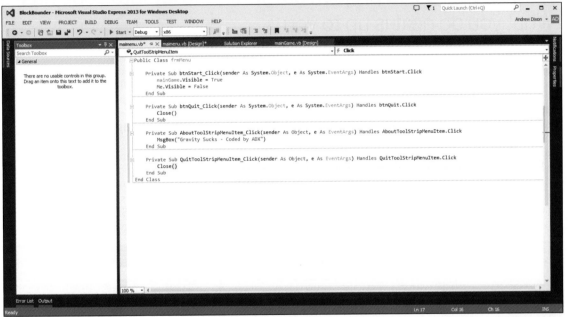

◀ Clicking on Quit will now close the game.

```
IntersectsWith(pctBottom2.Bounds) _
            Or pctBounder.Bounds.
IntersectsWith(pctTop1.Bounds) _
            Or pctBounder.Bounds.
IntersectsWith(pctTop2.Bounds) _
            Or pctBounder.Bounds.
IntersectsWith(pctFloor.Bounds) _
            Or pctBounder.Bounds.
```

```
IntersectsWith(pctCeiling.Bounds) Then

            tmrGavity.Enabled = False
            tmrMove.Enabled = False
            MsgBox("PlayerScore: " &
PlayerScore)

            If frmMenu.lblHighScore.Text
< PlayerScore Then
                frmMenu.lblHighScore.Text
= PlayerScore
            End If

            Me.Close()
            frmMenu.Visible = True
        End If

    End Sub
End Class
```

EXPERIMENT

Change the parameters of the If statement to suit your game, so that it increases difficulty by specifying certain boundaries of the PlayerScore variable. You could even add more ElseIf statements to have more boundaries: for example, 400 to 1000 = first speed increase, then 1000 to 1600 for second speed increase.

Where do you go next?

You might have completed the last project, but your journey into code has only just begun. What you do next is up to you

Congratulations! If you've made it this far, you're already developing a good working knowledge of how programs work, and you should be able to start programming your own apps and games. The best way to learn about programming isn't to learn a lot of theory or read a lot of books, although neither ever hurts. No, the best way to learn about programming is to keep coding. Sometimes you'll make something without any effort, and at other times you'll struggle and make mistakes. By learning how to fix problems and debug your own programs, you'll learn even

more about programming and discover ways to make your programs more efficient. The time and effort you put in is never wasted.

Mastering new languages

Now that you've had a taste of Scratch, Small Basic and Visual Basic, you might want to expand your talents to different platforms and devices. For instance, you may want to develop apps for mobile phones or tablets, or start working on desktop programs for MacOS X or Linux. Choosing what device and operating system you

▶ Python is now used in many schools and also professionally across a whole variety of industries.

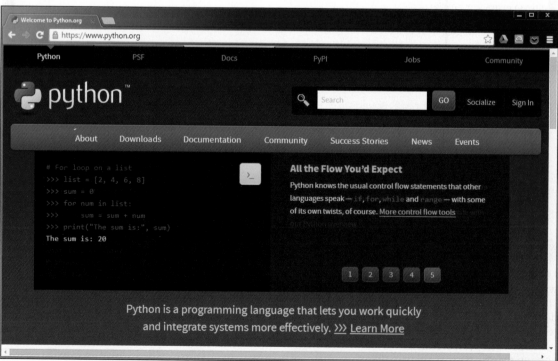

TOP TIP
Learning different languages will make you a very skilled and employable developer!

PROJECT IDEAS

To get better at programming, you need to practise, first writing simple applications, then working your way up to bigger programs and games. Here are some simple ideas for projects in Visual Basic using the skills that you've learnt from this book:

VISUAL CALCULATOR
Use the number buttons to enter values into the textbox, then include buttons for addition, subtraction, multiplication and division. See if you can mimic some of the popular functions you'd find on a calculator. The AC button should clear all boxes and variables. If you display the variables underneath the textbox, it makes testing a whole lot easier.

BINARY CONVERTOR
This project takes a standard (or denary) number and converts it into computer-friendly binary. See if you can work out how to do it.

VISUAL DICE
This bite-sized project creates a random number from 1 to 6, then displays the correct image for the dice roll. We covered producing random numbers earlier on. See if

you can remember where, then put that knowledge to good use. You can expand this to form different types of dice, which is great for virtual board and role-playing games.

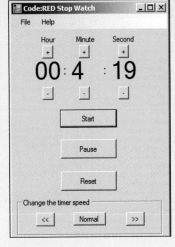

STOPWATCH
It might sound complex, but all this project needs to do is use a timer to count up or down on label boxes. Change the speed of the timer or set the initial time by using + and – buttons on hours, minutes and seconds. The Pause button should stop the Timer, and the Reset button should set all numbers back to 0 and the speed back to real time. You could even use a MsgBox to make alarms. Can you work out how to pull this off?

TEMPERATURE CONVERTOR
This project takes a number from the user and pastes it into one of two functions to convert between Celsius and Fahrenheit. The calculations for converting are simpler than you might think. The selection buttons

are called radio buttons and they have a Boolean value for on and off, which makes them easy to use with If statements.

WEAPON GENERATOR
This fun project creates random statistics for weapons in a video game. Working within certain boundaries, it can simulate the 'loot drops' you find in many action games and RPGs. Have fun with the name by having a list of adjectives and a list of nouns, such as animals, and randomly putting them together. High rolls could generate extra elemental damage.

want to develop on will determine which language to learn.

To develop for any Apple device, you'll need to learn a language called ObjectiveC. This language is based on the C style of programming, with some new features added by NextStep and Apple. To start coding, you'll need either a MacBook or an iMac and the Xcode software, which can be downloaded for free from the Apple store. Using Xcode, you can develop for the Apple desktop, mobile iOS phones and tablets. The only issues with ObjectiveC and Xcode are that they both have a steep learning curve, and to publish your applications on the Apple store you'll need

to be a registered Apple developer, which costs £60 a year.

The other major mobile platform is Android, and you can program applications using the Android SDK (Software Development Kit). You'll also need an Integrated Development Environment, or IDE, which provides you with all the tools and software you need to write and debug code. We'd recommend Eclipse, which is a powerful IDE that can be used with many different types of programming languages. The Android SDK and Eclipse will run on most major OS platforms, and more importantly, it can be downloaded for free at developer.android.com/sdk/index.html.

▶ Download the Java SDK and you can use Eclipse as an IDE.

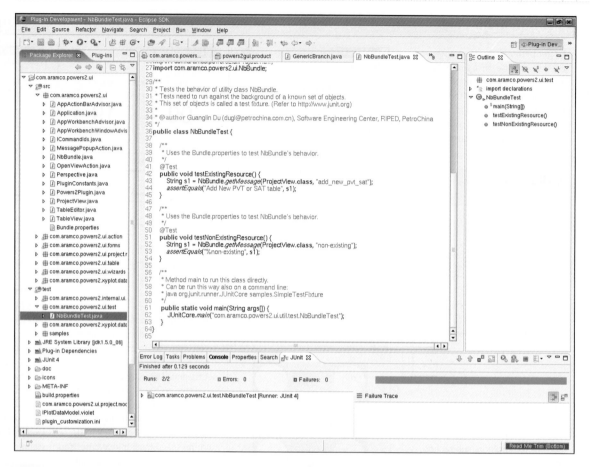

Coding for the web

HTML (HyperText Markup Language) is the code used to create web pages. It's not, strictly speaking, a programming language, but it's useful to know when developing internet-dependent applications and games. To view the HTML code of any website, you can find the View Source option in your browser, usually under the View menu. This will pull up a window showing all the code at work in your favourite websites. There are many types of software on the market to develop HTML, but as long as you have a text editor, such as Notepad, you can code using that and your internet browser will display the result.

Fancy making web games or interactive websites? JavaScript is a client-side language – it runs in your browser rather than on the server that powers the website – that's used primarily for internet browsers and webpages. It fits nicely into HTML to give your webpages interactivity and, just like HTML, you don't have to install software to get coding. If you want to work with a more fully featured IDE, several good ones are available for free. The syntax for JavaScript is simple to understand and, while the name suggests otherwise, it has nothing to do with the Java programming language.

Java and Python

Not that there's anything wrong with Java, one of the most popular cross-platform programming languages. The code can look complex, and it does have a steep learning curve. It takes much of its syntax style from C and C++, but if you can handle it you can make plenty of great games and apps for free. Simply download the Java SDK and you can use Eclipse as an IDE. To find out more about Java, visit docs.oracle.com/javase/tutorial/

If you want a more approachable option, try Python. It's now used in many schools and also professionally across a whole variety of industries. What seems like simple syntax quickly turns into a powerful cross-platform language that can create games and apps. The Python software is free to download and will work on most operating systems. The only confusing part is that there are two versions; the older version 2, which people still love and view as perfection, and the newer version 3, which attempts to modernise the language, but by doing that changes the syntax and commands.

There are plenty of other great languages that we don't have space to look at here such as PHP, C#, Ruby, PEARL, SQL and C++. Try googling them and do some research; you might find the perfect language for you!

PRACTISE CODING ON YOUR TABLET

If you have an iPad or Android tablet, there are some great free apps to practise coding techniques using your device:

HOPSCOTCH (iOS) is a free app that looks and behaves very similar to Scratch, where you have cartoon characters and drag your code in blocks onto the page. It's very simplistic, but really great fun for younger coders.
● www.gethopscotch.com

HAKITZU ELITE: ROBOT HACKERS (iOS and Android) is a robot fighting game that uses JavaScript syntax to move the robots and make them fight. It's a free app, but there are IAPs (in-app purchases) to disable ads and buy new parts for your robots.
● www.kuatostudios.com

CODE ACADEMY: CODE HOUR (iOS) is a free app that guides you through the basics of programming techniques such as data types, variables and If statements. Don't worry Android users, it will be coming to your platform soon.
● www.codecademy.com

CARGO-BOT (iOS) is a free puzzle game that really forces you to think logically and rewards the user for efficient looping with minimal code. The game was actually developed on the iPad with another app called Codea, which is a programming environment that uses another language, Lua.
● twolivesleft.com/CargoBot/

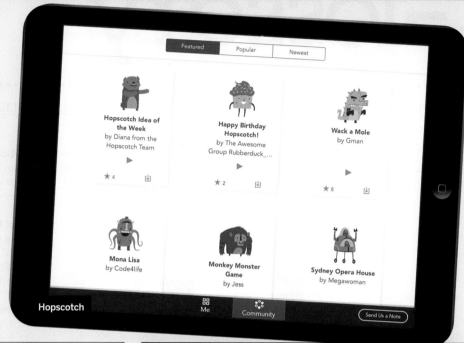

Hopscotch

Code Academy

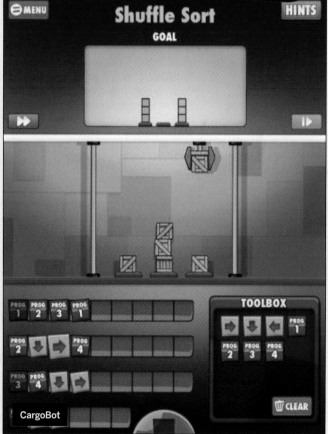

CargoBot

Hakitzu

Glossary

All those essential coding terms defined in plain English

Application: A complete program or a group of linked programs designed to perform a certain task or a set of tasks. While they're very different in what they do and how they're used, Adobe Photoshop, Google Chrome and Minecraft are all applications. Applications for smartphones or tablets are often described as apps.

Argument: A value or a reference to a value that's passed to a function, so that the function can do some work with it. If "sum" was the function in the instruction answer = sum (value1, value2), then value1 and value2 would be the arguments.

Array: A collection of values, strings or variables that can be accessed through an index number. When the program needs to access the information stored in the array, it just needs to call on the item by its index number.

BASIC: Beginner's All-purpose Symbolic Instruction Code. A high-level programming language designed with new programmers in mind, BASIC emphasises ease of use over performance, logical structure or sophistication.

Boolean: A value that has only two possible states: true or false.

C: A general-purpose, high-level programming language used widely in every area of software development. C is the basis for a whole family of popular languages, including C++, Objective-C and C#.

Class: The initial version of an object to be used in a program, which can then be used to create further instances. For example, you might define one circle as a class, then use that class to draw further circles.

Code: The lines of text or numbers that tell the computer what to do in a program. Code has to be written to conform to the specific style – or protocol – of a programming language.

Compiler: A program that takes the code written in a programming language and turns it into an application that other users can run and use.

Conditional: An instruction or statement in a program that's only run when a certain condition is met. For example, if the traffic light is green when your car reaches the lights, the car can go.

Control flow: The order in which instructions, function calls and statements are checked or executed as a program runs. Programmers use loops, subroutines and conditionals to affect how the control flow works.

Costume: In Scratch, a graphic that defines the visual appearance of a sprite. A sprite can have many costumes, and switch between them to express different states or simulate animation.

CPU: Central Processing Unit. The main processor in a computer, which runs the lion's share of the code in any application.

Debug: The process of checking through code, looking for a mistake that might stop a program running, or prevent it from running properly.

Function: A self-contained bit of code that performs a specific task, usually taking in some data, working with it and sending back a result.

HTML: HyperText Markup Language. The standard markup language used to create web pages. HTML code is processed by the browser, which then draws out and operates the page.

Instance: A single version or realisation of an object. The basic form of the object is defined by its class, but the instance might vary from this in any number of ways.

Instruction: An order given to the CPU by a computer program.

Integer: A whole number.

Interpretor: A program that takes the code written in a programming language and runs it line by line as an application without compiling it first. A program run in an interpreter won't be as fast as a compiled version, but has the advantage that it can be debugged or changed and run again without recompiling.

Java: An object-oriented, high-level programming language designed to run programs across as many computers as possible. Java is a hugely popular programming language, and used for many applications that run on the web.

JavaScript: A scripting programming language that shares some things in common with Java and C, and which is most commonly used in web pages and web-based applications.

Language: A language specifically designed to communicate instructions to a computer. Those instructions come in the shape of a program, written according to the syntax of that specific language.

Loop: A structure in a program that tells the processor to keep repeating one or more instructions, either forever, a specified number of times, or until certain conditions are met.

Object-oriented: A type of programming that focuses on objects (like a circle, a sprite or a menu), and on the data and behaviour attached to those objects. Object-oriented programs are theoretically more efficient, and easier to understand, maintain and adapt.

Operator: An object that manipulates values or variables. For example, a + or – symbol would be the operator in a sum.

Optimisation: The process of making a program work more efficiently and often at a higher speed.

Program: A series of instructions designed to perform a task on a computer, and written in a programming language. Programs have to be compiled or interpreted to be run.

Python: A general-purpose, high-level programming language that's designed to be highly efficient and easy to read. Python is a very popular language, and reasonably approachable to beginners.

Random: Something that's made or that happens without any pattern and can't be predicted.

Routine: A sequence of instructions that performs a specific task as part of a larger program.

Ruby: A general-purpose, high-level, object-oriented programming language. Ruby is designed to be efficient, easy to use and fun, based more on the way programmers think than the way computers operate.

Scratch: A simplified programming environment aimed at new programmers and especially young programmers. Scratch teaches the basics of programming without the user having to learn any actual code.

Script: A kind of program that tells an application, a web browser or an operating system what to do, line by line. Some programming languages specialise in scripting, and are designed to be easier to understand and use than other languages.

SDK: Software Development Kit. A group of programs that enable a programmer to develop applications for a specific operating system or device, such as a tablet, games console, computer or smartphone.

Source code: The code for a program before it's compiled or interpreted.

Sprite: In Scratch, an object that appears on the Stage and performs actions according to the blocks of script attached to it.

Stage: In Scratch, the area of the screen in which sprites move and operate according to their scripts.

Statement: The smallest standalone element of a program. Statements describe an action to be carried out.

String: A sequence of letters, words or numbers, stored by and used in a program. A string might be anything from a series of numbers to a word, a sentence or a larger chunk of text.

Subroutine: A routine within a routine. Subroutines are often used to handle tasks that might be needed again and again by a program.

Syntax: The structure of a programming language, and the rules that govern how the different instructions need to be written and laid out.

Toolbar: A horizontal or vertical bar containing icons that launch different tools in an application.

Value: A number, letter or symbol stored and used in a computer program. Values can either be constant, where they stay the same no matter what happens in the program, or variables.

Variable: A value that changes as a program runs its course. Variables aren't so much the value itself as the location that stores the value. The program can refer to the location by pointing to the variable, then use or change whatever value is held in it. ●

Resources

There are hundreds of websites where you can find tutorials, advice and support while you learn more about coding. Here are our favourites

www.w3schools.com
This site provides tutorials and reference for many of the big programming languages and tools used on the web. A good resource for information and education on HTML and JavaScript.

smallbasic.com/
Microsoft's SmallBASIC website isn't just the place where you can download the language, but a useful source of sample projects, tutorials and eBooks. Here, you can also find the SmallBASIC blog, which is full of useful hints and tips on the language.

www.khanacademy.org
Khan Academy teaches just about everything, but it also runs free courses in programming and computer science, with a JavaScript course that can take you all the way from simple drawing and animations to advanced natural simulations.

www.codeacademy.com
Code Academy is the best known of the specialist code schools, running courses in Ruby, Python, JavaScript and HTML. CodeAcademy was partly responsible for the computer science curriculum being used in many UK schools, and offers simple projects where you can learn a few coding skills in under half an hour.

www.kidsruby.com
KidsRuby is a simplified coding environment aimed at aspiring young programmers. It all works with real Ruby code, and you just write your code in one window and run it in another, so you can see exactly what any code you add or change does immediately. Colour-coded text makes it easy to use, and the team has started creating lessons and examples to help kids on their way.

www.kodugamelab.com
Part game, part visual programming environment, Kodu does a great job of introducing programming concepts while helping kids create their own simple games. It might not teach you how to code, but it does help teach computational thinking, and it's easy to use and fun. Versions for Windows 8, the Xbox 360 and earlier versions of Windows are available.

python4kids.wordpress.com/
A blog full of Python tutorials written by a programmer for his son. The tutorials work in Python 2.7 rather than the latest version, but they're easy to follow and provide a good background.

www.pygame.org
Pygame is a set of Python modules designed specifically for writing games, and one that makes the job of writing games in Python a whole lot easier. It's not designed specifically for kids, and you'll need python tuition elsewhere to make much out of it; a rough working knowledge is essential before you even start coding games. ●

Have fun and make games, or hack your homework using Ruby! Just tell your parents or teachers you're learning Ruby programming... ;)

Index

Teach Your Kids to Code

EDITORIAL

Editor: Stuart Andrews
Managing Editor: Priti Patel
Art Editor: Billbagnalldesign.com
Production: Rachel Storry
Contributors: Andrew Dixon

ADVERTISING & MARKETING

MagBook Advertising Manager: Simone Daws +44 20 7907 6617
Production Manager: Nicky Baker +44 20 7907 6056
MagBook Manager: Dharmesh Mistry +44 20 7907 6100

MANAGEMENT

Managing Director: John Garewal
Deputy Managing Director: Tim Danton
MD of Advertising: Julian Lloyd-Evans
Newstrade Director: David Barker
MD of Enterprise: Martin Belson
Group Managing Director: Ian Westwood
Chief Operating Officer: Brett Reynolds
Group Finance Director: Ian Leggett
Chief Executive: James Tye
Chairman: Felix Dennis

LICENSING & SYNDICATION

To license this product please contact Carlotta Serantoni on
+44 20 7907 6550 or email carlotta_serantoni@dennis.co.uk
To syndicate content from this product please contact Anj Dosaj-Halai on
+44 20 7907 6132 or email anj_dosaj-halai@dennis.co.uk